100
Reasons

100 true stories of the signs, wonders, and
miracles from a loving God.

Mary Genovese

All of the testimonies in this book are true, but some names have been changed to protect the privacy of individuals.

100 Reasons Copyright © 2018 by Mary Genovese.
All rights reserved
Published by ibelieve Publishers

Stuckonscripture.org

ISBN 9780692119549

Printed in the United States of America

Acknowledgements

I want to thank the people who made this book possible with their incredible testimonies! Your candid and transparent conversations take us on a journey from the heartwarming to the unexpected. Your experiences have encouraged and inspired us to believe in MIRACLES!

Special thanks to:

  Kenny, Christie, and Corey Campbell - my beautiful children. They inspire me to accomplish great things!

 Tony Genovese, a man with a big heart, and a desire to see this book succeed. He is a Computer Genius!

 Karen Weaver, my friend and fellow editor. Her compassion and love seep onto these pages.

Maria Friend, her friendship and computer savvy have been priceless.

Contents

Acknowledgements

Introduction

Birth of 100 Reasons

Let the Miracles Begin!

#1 HE ENCAMPS HIS ANGELS ROUND ABOUT ME

#2 HE WORKS THROUGH OTHERS TO HEAL US

#3 HE KNOWS JUST WHAT WE NEED

#4 HE GIVES US THE DESIRES OF OUR HEART

#5 HE IS MORE THAN A GOOD MAN

#6 HE GIVES US DIVINE ENCOUNTERS

#7 HE GOES BEFORE US

PRAYER OF SALVATION

#8 HE WORKS MIRACLES FOR ME

#9 HE HEALS US BODY, SOUL, AND SPIRIT

#10 HE PROTECTS US

#11 HE GIVES US MORE THAN WE ASK

#12 HE WAITS FOR ME

#13 HE WORKS IN MYSTERIOUS WAYS

#14 HE WRAPS HIS ARMS AROUND ME

#15 HE EMPOWERS US

#16 HE DOESN'T GIVE UP ON US

#17 HE SETS US FREE

#18 HE IS WITH US IN OUR SRTUGGLES

#19 HE MAKES ALL THINGS NEW

#20 HE TAKES CONTROL

#21 HE SAVES ME FROM MYSELF

#22 HE WATCHES OVER ME

#23 HE INVITES US INTO HIS KINGDOM

#24 HE CARES

#25 HE SINGS OVER ME

#26 HE CALLS ME FRIEND

#27 HE HAS A PLAN FOR ME

#28 HE SAVES THE NATIONS

#29 HE DOES WHAT DOCTORS CAN'T
#30 HE HAS KNOWN ME FROM A CHILD
#31 HE TEACHES US TO FORGIVE
#32 HE LEADS ME TO TRUTH
#33 HE MAKES ALL THINGS NEW
#34 HE SPEAKS TO US
#35 HE GIVES ME A VOICE
#36 HE HEALS ME
#37 HE IS BY MY SIDE
#38 HE GUIDES MY EVERY DECISION
#39 HE KNOWS MY NAME
#40 HE HEARS MY PRAYERS
#41 HE TEACHES ME TO LOVE
#42 HE DOES THE IMPOSSIBLE
#43 HE NUMBERS OUR DAYS
#44 HE BLESSES ME
#45 HE TOUCHED ME
#46 HE HEARS ME
#47 HE PROVIDES
#48 HE IS WITH ME
#49 HE SAVES
#50 HE CALMS MY FEARS

#51 – #60 TREASURE HUNTING

#61 HE NEVER LETS ME DOWN
#62 HE IS ALWAYS WITH US
#63 HIS AMAZING GRACE
#64 HE KNOWS MY PAIN
#65 HE BRINGS ME JOY
#66 HE IS WITH US IN OUR SUFFERING
#67 HE IS FAITHFUL
#68 HE'S GOT MY BACK
#69 HE CONNECTS US
#70 HE LEADS ME
#71 HIS WHISPERS ARE POWERFUL
#72 HE GIVES US STRADEGIES
#73 HE HEALS ME TIME AND AGAIN

3

#74 HE DOESN'T LET GO OF ME

#75 HE IS AWARE OF EVERYTHING

#76 HE WEAVES US INTO A TAPESTRY

#77 HE TEACHES ME HIS WAYS

#78 HE HAS A HEART FOR THE HOMELESS

#79 HIS WAY IS THE ONLY WAY

#80 HE PLACES THE ORPHAN IN FAMILIES

#81 HE PUTS WIND IN MY SAILS

#82 HE MAKES ALL THINGS NEW

#83 HE HAS FASHIONED AND FORMED ME

#84 HE IS MY STRENGTH

#85 HE MAKES ME SOAR

#86 HE HELPS ME FIND MY WAY

#87 HE IS SOVEREIGN

#88 HE RESTORES

#89 HE ANSWERS MY PRAYERS

#90 HE IS LOVE

#91 HE GIVES ME A NEW HEART

#92 HE CAN DO ANYTHING

#93 HE IS MY EVERYTHING

#94 HE TAKES ME INTO ETERNITY

#95 HE IS ALL I NEED

#96 HE IS MY GREAT PHYSICIAN

#97 HE HAS ALL AUTHORITY

THE 3 GREATEST MIRACLES OF ALL TIME...

#98 CREATION

#99 FORGIVENESS

#100 SALVATION

FINAL COMMENTS

Introduction

You might think that signs, wonders, and miracles need to be extravagant, and yes, sometimes they are. But what God wants you to know... is that first and foremost, He is present.

He is present in the big stuff, and in the small stuff.
He is present at this moment, and in the long-haul.
He is present in the everyday, and in the extraordinary.

He is present...

"Jesus Christ is the same yesterday, today, and forever."
Hebrews 13:8

The miracles you are about to read are not just isolated cases... they are available to all of us. Jesus desires to show up in your darkest hour, even more than you know. He also wants to surprise you when you least expect it... and shower you with good gifts.

But my hope is that you will look past these miracles, and be pulled into God's unexplainable love for you and me. He really does love us, and He wants to be loved by us too! Living for Jesus is not a religion, but it's a relationship. It is not based on fear, but on Love...

God has a plan for every one of our lives. You may not have taken that first step of asking Jesus into your heart, but when you do... your life will never be the same. God will start to show up in astonishing ways, just like He has for the people who have shared their testimonies with us.

If you want to know more about what it means to ask Jesus into your life, I have included pages devoted specifically to addressing this question (pgs. 32, 283). God has promised, that, not only has He given us abundant life through His Son Jesus, but that we have been given eternal life as well. Life does not end when we meet Jesus... it just begins! It is a relationship that lasts for eternity...

"For God so loved the world that He gave His only begotten Son, that whosoever believes in Him should not perish but have everlasting life. For God did not send His Son into the world to condemn the world, but that the world through Him might be saved." John 3:16, 17

The Birth of "100 Reasons"

As I thought about putting this book together, I was convinced that many people, like me, were holding onto some amazing testimonies! Our stories have the power to build faith and encourage hearts! I knew I wasn't alone, and I wanted to find others who would testify to the Greatness of our God! But I needed a push to get this book started. That push came when I heard the call to go to Israel. I caught wind of a monumental three day 24/7 worship gathering in the Holy Land scheduled to take place in October of 2018. I asked my friend Sonja to pray with me, and if God wanted me to write this book, and experience the land of Israel, then He would make it happen!

What has started out as a fundraiser to bring me to Israel, has quickly turned out to be so much more! I am overwhelmingly, undone by God's incredible love and faithfulness! This journey has just begun...

I knew I heard the call to go to Israel, but what happened next, took me by surprise. I saw this picture of Jesus extending His hand to me and

7

bidding me "Come... come and meet My family... worship Me in My homeland." I felt like a bride being beckoned by her Groom and excited to be introduced to His family. I know that sounds silly, but it was one of those intimate moments with God that has stolen my heart, and has caused me to believe that He has so much more in store for me as I take this journey to the Holy Land. As I am writing this sentence I am about 5 months away from taking this trip. I believe it is going to change my life forever. Thank you for purchasing this book, I believe your life will be changed forever too.

The testimonies you are about to read will make you laugh, cry, and at times shake your head in astonishment. Grab a cup of hot cocoa, and nestle into that cozy chair. As you turn these pages, watch God do what He does best... pour out His love upon us! He changes everything when He walks into the room. But don't just take my word for it, listen to what others have to say...

REASON # 1

HE ENCAMPS HIS
ANGELS ROUND
ABOUT ME

At the invincible age of 20 in 2006 I took a weekend road trip from San Francisco, CA to Portland, OR to visit a childhood friend from our home town of Buffalo, NY. Matt was an important and very special friend to me. I had the honor of leading him to the Lord back in high school. At a time when he was feeling discouraged by religion, especially Christianity in his life, he declared himself Agnostic. I wanted to know what that meant and why he felt that way. He was intrigued and wanted to know more about my faith too.

Later, through his extensive studies, open minded philosophies and incredible gift of teaching, he was now *my* spiritual teacher! Now a man of God with challenging questions, a non-judgmental lifestyle, and modern day parables that always kept me captivated and full of respect for him. He was a burly, jovial, poetic type. You could often spot him outside a coffee shop with a book in his hand, a tobacco pipe in his mouth, and a beret on his head.

Wanting to spend as much time with him as I could, I waited until the last possible minute to head back to San Francisco. This included driving thru the night with absolutely zero sleep, arriving around 6 am just in time to start my early hours at the bakery. As usual, I prayed for angels to protect me as I drove. "To camp themselves round about me. To be my rear guard and my front guard, side to side, that no weapon formed against me shall prosper", a prayer my mother (the author of this book) taught me growing up.

It was Christmas time and the highways were busy. A little over halfway home, at around 10pm, near Redding, CA, I ran into a pretty gnarly rain storm. Going 80 MPH in the fast lane in my little '95 Saturn in the dark, through a storm was a little concerning but I had no time for stopping. Andale! Adventurous, insane, opportunistic? You pick.

Singing along loudly to the radio, chugging red bull, and randomly clapping were my go-to ways to stay awake during long road trips. In the midst of this solo fiesta, I noticed a semi-truck driver to my right start to veer left into my lane with his blinker on and full determination with the rate at which he moved. I waited a second for him to see me and honked my unimpressive horn. He was still veering. With the chaos of the wind, the rain, and his probable distraction of peeling open a Slim Jim wrapper while sipping on a Big Gulp, he did not see me. Perhaps I was just in his blind spot.

Now we were both veering. Him towards me, and me away from him with nowhere to go but the large gravel median. The shocking bumpiness of the gravel jarred me into a panic state. I heard an echo of my brothers and father saying "whatever you do, don't slam your breaks when you're on gravel." Oops, too late. Some heavy fishtailing soon led to a full on spin out. My car

11

whirled around, going back onto the freeway I just came off of. It finally came to a full stop in the very center lane facing oncoming traffic, good choice! At record speed, cars zoomed past me on both sides. A few close calls and I gave up right then and there. I said, "This is how I die" aloud to myself with complete acceptance and almost amusement. There was so much activity all around me, I knew if I tried to turn off the road back on to the median, I would just get smashed from the side instead of the front, and die either way so what's the point in moving? Being a devoted Christian, I knew I was going to Heaven anyways and had full peace in my heart about death. The peace of God that surpasses all understanding resided in me in that moment.

Politely waiting to die, I felt invisible to other cars; no one even honking or swerving. Suddenly I felt my car being pulled backward in reverse. What? My car slowly and strategically drove backwards off the road, safely onto the median, and shut itself off. In complete disarray, now sobbing my hardest ever, I gasped aloud, "Jesus, Jesus, Jesus!" Intermittently followed by, "I didn't just do that!"

After about 10 minutes of crying, I was interrupted by red, white, and blue flashing lights and a knock on my driver's side window. Accusing me of trying to turn around in the median and getting stuck, I pleaded to the officer my case of getting ran off the road by a trucker and getting trapped in the middle of the freeway with cars on either side. With the rain now letting up a little, he asked me to get out of the car. Was he really about to make me do a sobriety test? Instead of walking a straight line with my finger on my nose reciting the ABC's backwards (which, let's be real, I can't even do that sober) he shown his flashlight on the side of my verrrrryyy dirty white (grey) car to reveal to me the obvious brush marks. "Are you *sure* no one hit you?" We walked to the other side, the same swooping brush marks were present. "Positive, nothing touched me." Dare I say to him what I so distinctly realized at that moment? That Angels had undoubtedly intervened like real life modern day Super Heroes to save my life? Noticing me in trouble, they shot over (or perhaps they are closer than we think) and pulled me backwards off the road. "Well, alright Miss, you be safe on those roads, have a good night."

I took pictures of my car that night. Evidence of Divine intervention. I still made it back in time to begin my shift as scheduled. I started telling people what happened. Most just gave a concerned look, followed by a, "wow, glad you're okay!" My boss, however, scoffed at me so as to ridicule my impossible accusations and walked away. That hurt my feelings. How could she not believe me? Surely I wasn't a crazy person, just someone excited about a beautiful miracle that just happened in my life. I was reminded of the Bible verse, "Don't cast your pearls to the swine." There will be people who will laugh at our testimonies, let them. With a smirk of inner joy on our faces and love in our hearts, we boldly share what God has done for us. Inside, I was disoriented about the fact I was still alive. I kept picturing coworkers finding out one by one that I had died last night in a car accident. Who was I to be kept from death and chosen to live? Wow, God must really, actually, truly have a plan for my life, a mission that has clearly not yet been accomplished. His angels are here to protect us, because only God knows when it is our time to leave this Earth.

Christie Marie Campbell

"For He will command His angels in regard to you, to protect and defend and guard you in all your ways" Psalm 91:11

13

REASON # 2

HE WORKS THROUGH OTHERS TO HEAL US

The account of Jesus healing the ten Lepers is found in Luke 17 of the Bible. As the story goes, only one of the 10 Lepers comes back to thank Him. It is not uncommon for Jesus to teach us through the actions of others, or even ourselves. In this next testimony this man comes back to give thanks for his miracle too!

In 2015 I was diagnosed with Fibromyalgia. It is a disease that is painful and effects the musculoskeletal system. The cause of it is not yet known. I had pain throughout my body, especially my shoulders. I had a hard time lifting my hands over my shoulders. This continued for a span of about ten months.

One day during a Wednesday night healing service, Pastor Jared Ruddy was preaching, and he was giving a testimony about a lady that was healed of an ailment while he was ministering to her. That night I was in much pain, but I decided to attend the service anyway. When he mentioned about that lady receiving a healing, I realized that the pain that I had was gone. I lifted my arms and there was no pain.

At the end of the service Pastor Jared asked if anyone felt that they had been touched by the Lord to come forward. I wanted to know for sure that what I received was genuine so I waited. The next day when I got out of bed the first thing I did was lift up my hands and there was no pain. I did that for a whole week and no pain.

Finally, I told Pastor Jim Ruddy my testimony. He had me give that testimony on a Sunday night service to encourage others. It's been almost 3 years now, and I've had no sign of Fibromyalgia. Praise God! I was under medication for those ten months to control the symptoms, but thanks be to God and Pastor Jared for bringing this word of healing to us.

Jose DeJesus

"I tell you the truth, anyone who believes in me will do the same works I have done, and even greater works, because I am going to be with the Father." John 14:12

REASON # 3

HE KNOWS JUST
WHAT
WE NEED

About 20 years ago when I was a single mom with two kids, my oven did not work. It actually hadn't worked for many months. It was time for me to get another oven, but I didn't have the money. I prayed about it for a while and I wasn't really sure what to do. And then one Saturday night when I was praying about it, God told me when you go to church tell somebody that you need an oven. I thought to myself, you can't be serious God. So in the morning when I went to church, I really wasn't planning on saying anything to anybody because I thought it sounded kind of crazy. So, after church I was standing in the narthex, and I heard God say to me tell somebody you need an oven. My thought was God, really? There was a man just standing next to me that I knew, Tony. So I looked at him and said to myself okay God. Then I looked at Tony, and I said "Tony I need an oven." He looked at me with a surprised but excited look on his face and said, "that's great!" My wife and I just bought a new oven yesterday and we don't know what to do with the old one. It still works. Then he said to me you go home and I'm going to go home and get the oven and bring it to your house and hook it up for you. I'm sure I stood there with my mouth wide open basically not believing what he had just said to me. But I did what he said, and about 20 minutes later he showed up at my house with an oven in the back of his truck. He brought the oven in, hooked it up, said God bless you and left. One thing that I remember was how excited he was to be able to bless me by giving me his oven. It was very obvious to me how God had not only blessed me with a free oven but he also blessed Tony by giving him the opportunity to bless me. I could hardly believe what God did that day. But the truth is that He's been faithful to me over and over again and never ceases to amaze me!

Kelly

"Ask a sign for yourself from the Lord your God; ask it either in the depth or in the height above." Isaiah 7:11

REASON # 4

HE GIVES US THE
DESIRES OF OUR
HEART

God is always faithful. Always, and He does give us the desires of our hearts.

As long as I can remember I have loved being around children. I taught Sunday school when I was in ninth grade, I just loved the innocence of little ones. When I graduated from school, I began teaching Pre-School. What an incredible age, although it could be totally trying at times. I know it was God's calling on my life, I would have had it no other way.

In the summer of 2005, I met the man that God hand chose for me. After many failed relationships, I knew this man of God was the one. Four years after we met and after a year engagement we were married. It was the most incredible day. We decided to give ourselves time to mesh into married life and just enjoy it being the two of us before starting a family. We figured within a few years, God would bless us with the gift of a baby.

In 2012, we were ready. Month after month for a year, nothing happened. We had thought several times I was pregnant but month after month we were disappointed with the outcome. In the summer of 2013, my OB-GYN sent us to an Infertility Specialist so we both could have a full work up. It was the most straining and exhausting process. After a few months of testing, the doctor told me my chances were slim. But he was going to get me started on Femara, which is actually used to treat different breast cancers, and could actually be effective for women with fertility issues. After doing research and seeing how many women became pregnant, we prayed and decided to opt for this. The side effects were not great. But, I was so desperate. In my heart, I figured God had this. Four months after being on this medication we still had no results. Not even a hint of pregnancy. I was devastated. So, heartbroken I continued to trust God and knew He had us covered. After meeting up with our specialist, he decided to keep me on the Femara but now we would add Artificial Insemination to the process. He told me it could be frustrating, he told me it could be an emotional roller coaster, he told me it may not work at all. But yet again, in my heart. God was just going to do this for us. So, we began doing all the necessary steps for this process. Everything the specialist told me was true, it was truly an emotional roller coaster. For months, I would lay on a table, go through a procedure with every hope in the world THIS time would be the time I became pregnant. Every time they did blood work at the office, my test came back negative. My entire attitude changed. I actually started to get mad-at God. I remember shaking my fists at Him, crying in the shower becoming angry at everything, not wanting to be around friends that were pregnant, as happy as I was for them, I could not understand why my prayers were being left unanswered. I felt like God was nowhere to be found.

One day while at work my temperature shot up to 104.9, after weeks of testing I was diagnosed with mono. A few days after my diagnosis I was supposed to head into the office for another insemination. When I called the office to verify my appointment, they told me they had to release me, they did not want to treat me while I had mono and to call them once I recovered. I hung up the phone and began to cry. I actually started to become so angry with God... Asking why He was doing this to us. As I sat on the floor, as clear as it could be, God asked me if I was going to trust Him or the specialist. I began to calm myself down, called my husband and told him I was done with treatments. That I was tired. He was so understanding and agreed it was too much for me. It was a lot for him too. But he knew how much I wanted this and he was so amazing. We squared off any remaining payments and moved on. I realized that I needed to trust God. He was not going to forget us and the desires of our hearts. What a weight lifted off of us. We began our daily lives without constant stress.

In September of 2015, I had noticed that I was overly tired and could not stand the smell of most foods. It went on for weeks, I chalked it up to a flu. On a cold Saturday I went to celebrate my friend, Tara's daughter's birthday. I could not even stay for the party, I just could not shake the flu. Before I left, she grabbed me a pregnancy test and sent me home with it. I really did not want to take it. I did not think anything other than having the flu. So, I came home and reluctantly took the test, and FIVE others as every test came back positive. WHAT?? I called Adam and he had no words. Days later we went to the doctor and it was confirmed. I was pregnant. BUT GOD... He did not forget me. He gave me exactly what I had asked for.

Adam, Amy & Eli

This verse is on my son's wall…

1 Samuel 1:27 "For this child we have prayed, and the Lord gave me the desires of my heart." He did. He really did. We welcomed Eli Nathaniel into our lives in May of 2016. So thankful for answered prayers. BUT God……

REASON # 5

HE IS MORE THAN
JUST A GOOD MAN

There is a starting point to every relationship, and when we meet Jesus for the first time, it is no different. Most of us can remember where we were... and how we met Him. Some have known Him from a child. Others, were introduced to Jesus after an invitation to church. But there is one thing that we have in common... we didn't choose Him - He chose us.

In fact He probably knocked on the door of our hearts repeatedly until we finally opened up and let Him in. It's called our day of visitation. The day Jesus enters our hearts and we are filled with His Holy Spirit. The day we say yes, the day we realize He's more than just a story, He's more than just a good man... He's the Savior of the world!

I had this encounter when I was about 28 years old. I was married, and a mother of three. I was living like everyone else at the time; for myself and for my family. The day "it" happened was just like any other day. I was not looking for anything, nor did I believe I needed anything. But that was all about to change. Life as I knew it would never be the same. This was the day I was going to meet Jesus. The day that God chose to reveal Himself to me. The day my life began...

Sitting on the front porch of my home, I was rocking in a chair watching my children play on a warm summer day. For some unknown reason, which is still a mystery to me, I got up off my chair, and went inside the house to a bookshelf where a dusty Bible sat for years. It was a gift from my dad given to me on my wedding day. But today was the day I was drawn to it. Today those pages were going to jumpstart me into an adventure of a lifetime. I reached for the Bible, headed back to my chair, and opened its cover. It was a surreal moment as I read the first sentence of the Bible "In the beginning God created the heavens and the earth." That's all it took! And the next thing I knew I was completely engulfed in the presence of God! I began to weep uncontrollably, and my soul just flooded with an unbelievable sense of God's presence and love. I was very aware that God had just entered me. I felt ridiculously different. I felt healed, set free, and empowered with boldness.

My thoughts all turned towards God... who He was, who I was, and what was going on in the world around me. I realized for the first time that I knew nothing about God. I realized that I had been in the dark all of my life. My perception of God was all wrong. I realized for the first time, that I had been lied to by the enemy. I was furious! It felt like I had to make up for lost time. I had an incredible zeal to tell people the truth about God, and to defend Him. He was everything I ever needed! He was loving... He cared. Everything I had previously thought about God was a lie, and the scales fell from my eyes. I could see Him for who He really was for the first time. I felt the reality of what it meant to know Him, and His love for me. We were definitely in a relationship now. He wasn't a far-away entity. For the first time in my life I felt alive! Just 24 hours earlier I was minding my own business, and going through the motions of everyday life, but today my life had been radically changed! I was headed on a journey to know my Father in heaven. His invitation was more than intriguing, it was like winning the lottery... I felt like a million bucks!!

Just to be clear, I believed in God all my life, but it was on this day that I really understood what it meant to *know* Him. He was now living inside of me, and I was born of the Spirit. This was way different from just knowing about Him. I had been radically changed by this new revelation that had seemingly come out of nowhere, and blind-sided me!

Reading the Bible is how I first met Jesus, so I continued to read it until I finished it completely. It's like this... until we read this book, we only know partial truths and have a limited understanding of who He is. It just makes sense that if we want to know the truth about God that we would start by reading His Word. I've read the Bible 28 times since then. It is truly the air I breathe. The only way I can describe how I feel when I'm reading the Bible, is that it feels like home. God is with me. It's the best part of my day... it's our meeting place. He speaks to me...

So if you are questioning your purpose in life, or wondering if God even exists, then I want to encourage you to ask Him. I am pretty sure He's been trying to get your attention for a while now, and maybe reading this book is just one of those ways. I guarantee you won't be disappointed, in fact you'll probably be asking yourself why you waited so long! He is wanting to be in a relationship with you. God is love, so don't be afraid. His goodness will lead you to truth and set you free. Pick up a Bible today and ask God to reveal Himself to you... He will. I also would encourage you to find a Bible believing church to help teach you, pray for you, and welcome you as family. We've all been on both sides of the tracks… come home. This could be the first day of the rest of your life. Some things just can't wait… this is one of them.

Mary Genovese

"The thief does not come except to steal, and to kill, and to destroy. I have come that they may have life, and that they may have it more abundantly." John 10:10

The verse above has been my "Life-Verse" since the day I met Jesus – it has revolutionized my Life!

I pray my book will draw you closer to God, and that you will know just how much you are Loved!

REASON # 6

HE GIVES US DIVINE ENCOUNTERS

You may have heard of the saying, "God works in mysterious ways," well, it's true! I believe this next testimony will catch you by surprise. You can be walking through life, minding your own business, doing your own thing, when boom! God sets up a divine encounter that you won't forget for a long time. Our next testimony is just one of those encounters...

While leaving Roswell Cancer Institute in Buffalo, NY I saw this tall, lanky, young man, across the street running over small snow mounds heading towards the car ramp. When I saw him, one word came to me, "Share." I knew that was the Lord letting me know I was to share the Gospel with him. I have to admit, my first thought was, "Oh, no!" You see I was carrying my purse, and heavy equipment after a performance with my piano/voice students at Roswell. I said, "Lord, if You want me to do this. You're going to have to slow him down and keep him in his car until I find him." You see I'm just 4'10" with short legs. So, I picked up my speed and found where he was. He was right by the entrance, just a little ways from my car. I placed the equipment in my trunk, and I went over to his car. I motioned for him to roll down his window. He did.

His car was running and the song on his radio was playing, "Lean on Me." I thought… well, this is a good start! I opened by saying, "Jesus loves you!" His reply? "I'm Buddhist." I prayed inwardly, "God, please give me the words." Instantly, He did, and I blurted out, "You know, Buddha is dead but Jesus is alive!" He got out of his car and said, "You know, it's funny you should say that." Then, he showed me a picture on his phone of a woman in a hospital bed with a big cross on the wall behind her. He told me that woman was his wife, a patient at Roswell. I said, "This is awesome that there is a cross in her room!" He replied, "You don't understand, there is no cross on that wall." Wow!

I then shared the love of God with him. He received the Lord right there in the parking lot as his wonderful Savior! God is so good! I encouraged him to share the Love of God with his beautiful wife, and I prayed with him for her healing. We hugged, then I went to my car and left. I never saw that young man again. But I thank God for that unexpected encounter. Oh, Lord, thank you for giving me the opportunity to be obedient to your voice and share your love with him!

Pat Petersen

"There is no other name (Jesus) under Heaven given among men by which we must be saved." Acts 4:12

27

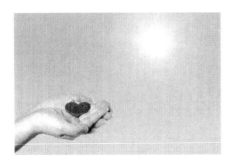

REASON # 7

HE GOES
BEFORE US

At 29 years-old, I planned to attend a women's retreat in California, but I purchased the plane ticket for the wrong week. This meant I would have to miss the retreat or change the flight. When I called to change the flight, I was told that I would have to pay the difference of $350 when I checked in. This was before cellphones and ticket machines. I was nervous. As a student, I didn't have much cash flow. I would have to use my spending money on the flight! I prayed and fasted.

On the day of my departure, a storm hit, a storm so fierce it knocked the power out at the airport. All flights were being canceled. I called the airport, and the attendant told me, "If you get down here right now, we'll get you on the last flight, but you must come now." Without a minute to spare, she got me on the flight with a handwritten boarding pass. When I arrived in Chicago, I went to retrieve my boarding pass to California. "Oh," the attendant said, "You have a fee of $350 for changing your flight." "Yes," I answered and reached for my cash. "We are going to waive the fee because you jumped on an earlier flight out due to the weather." Coincidence? Or a merciful God who even has the power to change the weather for us. He tenderheartedly taught me that if I would just "ask, I would receive."

Laurie

"So I say to you, ask, and it will be given to you; seek, and you will find; knock, and it will be opened to you." Luke 11:9

SALVATION

It is the starting point for all believers. The day that Jesus enters into our lives and changes us forever. The day the "lightbulb" goes on! The day this world, and its cares, just seem to fade away in light of this new revelation - "JESUS LOVES ME!"

"We love Him because He first loved us." 1 John 4:19

When you come to the understanding, that Jesus is real and that He came to this earth to save you, then you have understood the greatest revelation of all times! When you are ready to talk with God, there is no formal prayer that saves you… but it is your faith, believing that Jesus died on the cross, and conquered sin, hell, and the grave, to reconcile you back to God. The Bible tells us in Romans 10:9 that if you confess with your mouth the Lord Jesus, and believe in your heart that God has raised Him from the dead, you will be saved.

"Behold, I stand at the door and knock. If anyone hears My voice and opens the door, I will come in to him and dine with him, and He with Me." Revelation 3:20

The Sinner's Prayer

Dear God, I acknowledge that Jesus is the Son of God. I believe that He died on the cross, that His blood was shed for my sins and that He arose from the grave and conquered death. I understand that I was born a sinner and that I have sinned by disobeying Your commandments. I ask You to forgive me for these sins. Please change my heart to be like Yours – loving and full of forgiveness. Help me to know You more. Help me to find a Bible believing church, and bring people into my life who can help me on this new path. Be my Savior. Be my Lord. Thank You for saving me from death and giving me new life. Amen.

REASON # 8

HE WORKS
MIRACLES FOR ME

Over my bed on the wall I have the quote, "Everyday Holds the Possibility of a Miracle".

Let me tell you about one of the best I've personally experienced.

In 1969, I was a senior in high school, the daughter of middle class conservative Catholics from a small town in central New York State. In spite of my upbringing, I became pregnant by spring of that year. Back then, sex outside of marriage and illegitimacy had a huge stigma and I knew no one else who this had happened to. My boyfriend left me alone with this situation and I was terrified to tell my parents. Honestly, I would have done *anything* to avoid telling them. Abortion (thankfully) was not legal, nor easily accessible back then, or I might have taken that route to solve the problem of my untimely pregnancy. My older brother Bob was going to move me to New York City to deliver and surrender there, but ended up having to marry his girlfriend who became pregnant by him. In the end, at 4 months along, with every door closed to me, I told my parents. It was the worst night of my life! My mother screamed, accused and reacted much as I had expected. My dad, well, he didn't say much until the next day. For the first time in my life that I could remember, he told me he loved me. Too little, too late; I needed to hear that, years before. The next thing I remember was being taken to confession to a priest in another town. God forbid our priest would know my sin and our family shame! He recommended a couple of Catholic homes for unwed mothers where I could be hidden away until after I delivered my child. We decided on Our Lady of Victory in Lackawanna as I had an older sister living in Buffalo. Arrangements were made and I was whisked away with an elaborate story of where I was and the new job I had. When I didn't go home for Christmas that year, family and friends thought I was on a skiing trip in Minnesota. My younger siblings were never told before or after that I had a baby. The shame and guilt were overwhelming!

For five months I resided along with 49 other girls/women in a maternity home where we used fake names and pretend wedding rings if we went out into the public. Our "counseling" consisted of being told that if we loved our babies we would surrender them for adoption to a good loving two parent family. Social services were never offered as an option to keep our children. Few left with their babies. We were not good enough, nor most able, to raise them on our own and many like me, did not have family support. We were told the same lie then that is told to girls/women today who abort, that this will solve your problem and you can go on with your life as if it never happened. Your life is never the same! Once a girl/woman becomes pregnant, she has a child and is a mother; neither abortion nor surrender changes that. All the denial, alcohol or other numbing agents in the world do not make the guilt or regret go away. I buried the pain of losing my son for years. God brought an amazing man to be my husband (another testimony for another time) and three more sons to me, but after several years, while training for a pro-life pregnancy hot line, the lid came off and the pain came pouring out. I didn't know where to go for help. I tried the agency that my baby was placed through, the Church and Erie County. I was repeatedly told I was the only one with these issues. I knew no other birthmothers. It wasn't something anyone shared about themselves. Finally, after some time I found a support group for people with adoption issues. All members of the triad (adult adoptees, birthparents and adoptive parents) were welcome. There I met other women like me, who had delivered their children hidden away in homes for unwed mothers and relinquished them, often against their wills. My pain was their pain. I also met adult adoptees who had many questions about whom they were and where they came from. Many wanted, at the very least, medical information and there were also a few brave supportive adoptive parents. In an era of closed adoption with sealed records, little information was shared. Many in the group were searching for their lost family members, but me......I was just trying to validate my own feelings and trying to heal. I could not, would not search for my son. I had been told I would ruin his life if I ever tried. I did, however, know a lot more medical information about my family than I did when I filled in forms 25 years prior. So I updated my **non**-identifying medical information with the agency that placed my son. I also located his birthfather who now lives in Florida, wrote him explaining the questions that the adoptees I met had and asked him to update as well. He was more than willing and sent his info to me which I forwarded to the agency. At the advice of the support group leader, I asked them to acknowledge receipt of the medical information and to tell me when they sent it to the last known address of my son as they had done with mine three months before. Shortly after this my husband and I went away for the

34

weekend. Upon returning, I did notice in the stack of mail an envelope from my adoption agency. I didn't open it until that evening along with the other mail thinking it was just an acknowledgement that they received and had forwarded my son's birthfather's non-identifying medical update. As I read the letter it made reference to "your son Michael". I had named my son Robert; therefore, I thought there was some mistake. Oh, there certainly was!!!!! As I looked more carefully at the inside address, I realized someone had made a huge error. The letter that was supposed to go to my son via his parents had come to me and as it turned out, the letter for me went to them. I had my son's name and address sitting in front of me and mine was with him. Neither of us had searched nor would have left on our own. God knew this and had other plans.

One couple in my group had been actively searching for their daughter, whom they were forced to surrender, for 35 years. I was afraid to tell them of my blessing. Another woman in the support group who was a professed atheist proclaimed, "That was God!" No one could believe it. They were all so happy for me.

There is so much of this story that I am not including, but want to say that my son Mike and I have had a great reunion. I know his mom and dad and my husband and I are Grandma and

35

Grandpa to his son. I believe this all was a miracle! I Still pinch myself and ask, "Why me God?" I was told by a professional searcher that with the type of closed adoption we had it would be next to impossible to ever find him. Meeting Mike has been very bittersweet. I am his mother, but not his mom. However, over the years, God has been healing the pain, the hurts, the rejection and shame. After years of secrets and lies, shame and loss, I am free! Because I know the love and forgiveness of Father God through His Son Jesus, I can walk in my truth with my head held high and rejoice that the son I never thought I'd know on this side of Heaven is only a phone call away!

Mary LaLonde Fay

"For I know the thoughts that I think toward you, says the LORD, thoughts of peace and not of evil, to give you a future and a hope." Jeremiah 29:11

REASON # 9

HE HEALS US
BODY, SOUL, AND
SPIRIT

Many years ago, I had the opportunity to share the Gospel with a young woman renting an apartment from my parents. They had been sharing with her about the goodness of God and reaching out to her in practical ways. I sat across from her, knee to knee, as I shared God's plan for salvation with her. She had many needs in her life, including a need for healing. Her eyes were swollen and discolored. She looked at me through two tiny slits, desperately ready for God to intervene in every area of her life.

As we held hands and bowed our heads, I had the privilege of leading her through the "Sinner's Prayer" and hearing her ask Jesus to come into her heart and transform her, from the inside-out. We prayed for God to intervene even further, in several situations she was facing. When we squeezed hands and said "amen," I looked up and could see the Lord had healed her, instantly! The swelling and discoloration of her eyes was completely gone! Big, bright eyes full of hope and amazement glowed back at me. She marveled as she looked in the mirror at the evidence of God's healing. She was confident that, if God could heal her body, He could heal her broken family. Thanks be to God!

"Now to Him who is able to do exceedingly abundantly above all that we ask or think, according to the power that works in us." Ephesians 3:20

REASON # 10

HE PROTECTS US

As Psalm 46:1 assures us, "God is our refuge and strength, an ever-present help in time of trouble." I find it amazing how, one minute, we can be going about our daily routines and the very next minute our lives can take a 360 degree twist! Yet, God is always right there...the Omni-present, Omniscient One...*always* and in *all ways* on alert and ready to intercede on our behalf. He dwells with us. God is the unseen guest at our tables, our invisible guardian...always there...just in the *nick of time!*

One Sunday, while I was getting ready to attend our 7pm church service, my wife said she was going to set the oven on self-clean. Usually, she'll leave the kitchen and move to the front room, to avoid smelling all the fumes. But this time was different because she noticed the church bulletin on the kitchen table. So, she sat down at the kitchen table to read it. Usually, she reads it earlier in the day. But today was one of those days when timing would be everything. Positioned near the stove, her eye caught sight of an intense flame burning inside the oven! Immediately, she turned off the oven and was able to stop the flames from getting out of control. I know God was with us that day, as He is every day, because He surely saved us from what could have been a huge disaster!

Wayne

"I will abide in Your tabernacle forever, I will trust in the shelter of Your wings. Psalm 61:4

REASON # 11

HE GIVES US MORE
THAN WE ASK

Nick had been out of work for eleven months, from the beginning of February 94 to the end of December of that same year. We were living on a fraction of his typical paycheck. For those months we struggled to make ends meet just getting by. But by January of 95 he went back to work, and we began to feel the heavy pressure of unemployment lift. Soon after Nick had gone back to work we received in the mail an adjusted electric bill that was undeniably extreme in our eyes. It could have been a million dollars owed and it couldn't have pelted us any harder than receiving that shocking statement demanding a payment of $1180. The urgency of this bill stated that our payment was OUTSTANDING and OVERDUE. Ouch! This bill was the very last thing we needed after eleven months out of work.

The utility company stated that we had gone more than two years without an actual meter reading. Their records indicated that we had been estimated for that period of time and they accused us of flipping our electric meter. We had never heard such a thing. My husband and I groaned and lamented this bill, but by the grace of God I turned my heart towards the Lord and I brought this burden to Him in prayer. Recognizing that we needed help I called out to God in my heart I cried, "O my Father, my Lord, help us! My God, we need you! We have no way to meet this need; show us the way, show us what to do! Please, help us! Instantly, from deep within I felt the Spirit of God stir and rise up out of my heart, (every cell in my body felt Him stirring) as He answered my heart's cry saying, "Sherry," He called my name, He got my attention, "Sherry! My God shall supply all of your need according to his riches in glory." I remember the exhilaration within me as my entire body felt this word! I felt the weight of His word; I actually recognized and knew that this was our answer. I couldn't hold it in! I excitedly conveyed what I had just heard to my husband, "Nick!! I just heard the Lord speak unto us, He said, "My God shall supply all of your need according to His riches in glory!"

With jubilant excitement I bounced all over the kitchen and dining room rejoicing in the word that I heard the Lord speak! I could barely contain my joy! Nick was thrilled for a moment, it sounded great, and he liked the concept, but in a matter of moments his mind went naturally to the practicality of the word. How? How is God going to meet this need? When is He going to accomplish this? Where is He getting the funds? Every question escalated the reality of my comments as being absurdly impossible. I had no way of answering such questions. I had no idea how God was going to meet this need. Without answers, each question felt like a punch to the gut, a slap to the side of the head. How exactly is God going to do this? I know my husband didn't realize it, but his words carried the bitter bite of the enemy. That devious instigator and enemy of man, whose sole intent was bent on stealing the word I had just received from the Lord. Very distinctly, I remember the urge I felt to defend God and to take matters into my own hands. I stormed around the kitchen verbally building up my case, building up my argument against the electric company. "Well then, I will just call Niagara Mohawk and I will tell them that we did not flip our meter and that we should not be held responsible for this. We should not be forced to pay this outrageous bill! That's it! I told Nick, I am calling the electric company! God will meet our need! That is exactly what I did, I took matters into my own hands; I called the utility company. I reached the recorded message maze until I finally reached a live person. I spilled out my rehearsed complaint and expressed all of my frustration to the woman on the other end of the line, half confident, half expecting God to do something spectacular.

The woman from Niagara Mohawk apparently was having a very bad day and I must have pushed her to her breaking point! She came back at me with a vengeance! She yelled, screamed, and decreed, "You flipped your stinking meter! You owe it, you are not getting out from under this, you are going to pay every last cent of this bill!" You owe it! You will pay it! It's due now! We want this payment now!…" Embarrassed, and defeated, I felt like an absolute idiot for stepping out in what I thought was God's way of meeting our need. I forced myself to turn to the Lord with my brokenness of heart. I cried, Lord, forgive me for overstepping my bounds, for taking matters into my own hands. I know I heard You speak this word to me. Help me; lead me; show me the right steps…. Instantly I felt the Spirit of God stir and rise up out of my heart and declare to me a second time, "Sherry, my God shall supply all of your need according to His riches in glory by Christ Jesus; Sherry, I will supply all of your need." O my God! I replied, Thank you! Thank you! Thank you! I don't know how You are going to do it, but I believe it! I believe You! I believe Your word to me! In my heart I knew the voice of God was speaking loud and clear. I knew at that very moment the need was met! When GOD spoke, something inside of me shifted, it was settled! I can't really explain it, but it was done. We still owed the $1180.00; but in my heart where I heard the voice of GOD promise to meet our need, I knew it was accomplished.

Two long weeks passed and nothing has changed. By this two week point Nick wanted to see some progress in this issue. In retrospect, it is obvious now, that the enemy was putting intense pressure upon him to DO something; DO anything; STOP ignoring this looming bill. I finally came up with what seemed to be a brilliant idea! I know, I will call Niagara Mohawk and I will tell them straight out, it took them two years of neglecting the meter reading of our bill, and just estimating it, so they can take two years of payments to recoup this outstanding amount. That's it! I calculated it on the calculator, twenty four months divided by $1180 equals $49.16 extra per month for the next two years. It seemed reasonable; it sure was a whole lot better than paying a lump sum that we did not have. I called the utility company again. I tapped into the endless recorded message cycle, till finally without being able to speak to a living person, the utility company gave me the option to pay this bill in installments. Their only option came out to three payments of $393 each. My excitement came crashing down with the hard reality of their choice. That was way too much! Add to that our average monthly bill and that is close to $500 for those months. We were still feeling the pinch of my husband's time off of work.

The recorded message on the other end of the line kept repeating choose number one for yes or, choose number two for no. Choose one for yes, choose two for no. I was in turmoil; this payment was way too much, our budget could not handle it at this time. I was sick. The pressure was mounting. I began to pray. "O my Father, what should I do? Is this Your answer? Is this what You have for us? Help me, show me!! You said that you would meet all of our need according to Your riches in glory!!" Choose one for yes, the recorded voice repeated on, choose two for no. In my heart I cried out, "Father!! What should I do? I trust You, show me!!" Immediately I heard in my heart the soft gentle voice of the Lord as He whispered to me, "Sherry, my God shall supply all of your need!" Hallelujah! I knew, this choice is not it! This is not how God would supply our need. I hung up the phone knowing that these payments were not what the Lord had for us! I was so blessed so excited that the Lord would grant me wisdom. This choice was a compromise. That extra $393 a month would have been brutal! I didn't know how, nor did I know when, but I knew the Lord would supply all of our need according to His riches in glory!

Two more weeks come and go, so it has been a solid month since we first received that past due bill. It is a solid month since I heard the Lord respond to my heart cry for help. On this unsuspecting day while my husband was at work, the children were at school and I was sitting at the kitchen table about lunchtime reading my Bible when I felt the Spirit of the Lord rise up out of my heart and I heard Him say, "Call them now." I knew very matter-of-factly that He was talking about Niagara Mohawk. I got up from the table to get the phone and called the same number that I had called twice before regarding this bill, but this time instead of the dreaded recorded message immediately there was a beautiful sing song-y voice on the other end of the line.

I didn't say a single word, I didn't have to. The sweet voice on the on the other end did all the talking. Hmm! HmmMMM! Humph!

Click, click, click; click, click, click; click, click, click....I could hear the sound of the keyboard clicking, typing away as the voice graciously spoke saying, "Oh! How I hate when they do things like this! They shouldn't do this, this just isn't right! Humph! Click, click, click; click, click, click; click, click, click.... Hmm! She did not ask me anything, and I didn't offer any information. The voice broke in through the clicking of the keyboard and said, "There! It's done! Click, click, click... You don't owe that anymore! It's gone! Click, click, click; click, click, click; click, click, click....I started holding my breath afraid my breath would chase this new reality away! Tears welled up in my eyes; my heart was bursting with overwhelming joy ecstatic at the greatness of God! Oh wait! Wait just a minute! she stated with delight. Click, click, click; click, click, click; click, click, click. "Ah yes! That's better. As a matter of fact," she said, "you now have a $237 credit! Yes! That's much better! Yep! $237 to your credit!" Holding my breath, as quietly as I could I began jumping up and down praising the Lord for not only supplying my need, but meeting it exceedingly abundantly above all that I asked or thought! I turned to the Lord in our time of need and He supernaturally led me and met our need! He canceled our debt and blessed us with a surplus. He led me through the enemy's attempt to steal my word, and his attempt to get me to compromise the word. God is so good! He is faithful to His word and a rewarder to those who put their trust in Him! I didn't have to Do anything but believe. Glory Hallelujah!

Sherry Jankowski

"And my God shall supply all your need according to His riches in glory by Christ Jesus." Philippians 4:19

REASON # 12

HE WAITS FOR ME

Growing up, I came from a large family; eight of us in all. I was surrounded by many friends whom I shared all of life's experiences with, including school, boy scouts, little league baseball, and just plain hanging out. Alcohol was something that was accepted in each of our families and considered a normal part of our lives. At age thirteen I started drinking, and at fourteen I was smoking marijuana.

Though I made some bad decisions, I was a good kid, grew up in the Catholic Church, and understood who God, Jesus, and the Holy Spirit were. When I was a teenager, I remember asking God this question: Why are we here, what is the purpose, and the meaning of life? Do we just go to school, graduate, get married, have children, work the rest of our lives and then die? Is that it? There had to be something more. Looking back I can't help but feel the Lord wanted to answer these questions, if I would have just opened the door of my heart and let Him in.

At the age of eighteen, I enlisted in the United States Navy and served four years. When I returned home I found things had not changed much. I picked up right where I left off, but now I was "legal." When I was in my mid-twenties, I started to use cocaine. It was part of a lifestyle I lived for many years. The frequency of alcohol and drug consumption increased and we were having the time of our lives. We were young and had our whole lives ahead of us. Life was one big party. This continued for many years, and again I found myself wondering if this is what life was all about.

There it was again, that sense of something knocking on the door of my heart, my life. Finally, I had enough. I became sick and tired of being sick and tired. Living with hangovers on a regular basis, living a life of defeat and despair. No hope, no future, nothing but emptiness. The party was over. I had nowhere to turn. Friends and family denied my attempt to reach out to them, and they didn't see that anything was wrong. In my mind I was alone, sitting in a room by myself with empty beer cans, bottles of alcohol, cocaine residue on the tables, and ashtrays with piles of cigarette butts. It was a bad place to be and I wanted out. Thoughts of suicide started to enter my mind. I hated myself, I hated life. This had to end.

As I sat there alone in that virtual "party room" in my mind, I was at my lowest point of depression and despair when suddenly there was a knock, a knock at the door of my heart. Could that be Him after all these years? Is He still there? I opened the door of my heart and Jesus stepped into the room. He wrapped His arms around me and I buried my head into His shoulder and cried. On August 29th 2000, I opened the door and I asked Jesus into my life. After all that time, He never left. He waited patiently outside the door of my heart until I was ready. I now belong to Him. Since that time, I have been delivered from that lifestyle. My eyes have been opened to see what is possible in this life He has given us. A life of purpose and promise, a life of hope, and best of all, a life that is yet to come, an everlasting life so incredible words cannot describe it. The best is yet to come!

Joe

"Here I am! I stand at the door and knock. If anyone hears My voice and opens the door, I will come in and eat with him, and he with Me."
Revelation 3:20

REASON # 13

HE WORKS IN
MYSTERIOUS WAYS

I was brought up Catholic and remained that way for many years. One night a group of us were driving back from a work event which didn't go very well. As we were driving we were cussing and complaining about the trip. I felt somewhat depressed and really just wanted to get out of the car and crawl into bed. As we drove I noticed a car pass us by with a bumper sticker that said WDXC 99.5. That was the whole sticker, no words. But I remembered it for the next hour and a half as we drove back to Buffalo. It's as if I was being drawn to it.

When I got into my own car the first thing I did was tune to 99.5 and I heard this southern voice which I would learn was Dr. J Vernon McGee. The program was called "Through the Bible" and immediately his voice pulled me into an interest level which I had never had before. As I heard more of the Word I wanted to get my own Bible. I found Benders Christian Store in Williamsville and the good people there helped me to pick out my first Bible.

As I read the Bible, I would say this is when I fell in real Love with Jesus. I was no longer reading an old book from my religion instructions days. This book was speaking to me, I became part of the story and felt the Power and Love of God. I Love going to church now and being part of a corporate group worshiping the

King of Kings. I also Love to Love Him in private. He is my God, My Friend, and the lover of my soul. I'm not sure why I noticed a bumper sticker and then remembered it for another few hours, but I am sure glad I did. It changed my life!

So, if someone makes fun of your Jesus stickers or if you feel you haven't lead someone to Christ, don't be discouraged. There is a person who drove around in a car with a WDCX 99.5 bumper sticker 30 years ago that lead me to Christ! I was never was able to thank them, but I was able to thank God.

Tony

"Purify me from my sins, and I will be clean;
wash me, and I will be whiter than snow." Psalm 51:7

REASON # 14

HE WRAPS HIS ARMS
AROUND ME

I was laying on the bed in the middle of my room sobbing. I had just suffered a bad break-up, and it stung. I couldn't find words, and I certainly couldn't find the motivation to get out of bed, much less reach out to any friends who might be able to comfort me during this time. So I laid there and just kept sobbing. I felt rejected, depressed, and ultimately – alone. I had a worship song playlist that my sister had put together for me playing in the background to drown out my crying, and for a brief moment I focused on the words to the song playing at the time – something about being wrapped in the arms of the Father. It was in that moment that I experienced the miracle of His presence. I felt His arms wrap around me and give me a hug that felt so real I could have sworn that someone else had been present in the room with me and snuck up behind me to give me a hug. And then I felt the most supernatural feeling of warmth envelope me. At that moment, I knew that it was God comforting me as I laid there in tears, and I remembered the words from Psalm 34:18: "The Lord is near to the broken-hearted, and saves those who are crushed in spirit."

I have never experienced His presence like that since, and perhaps I never will. But what I do know is that at my lowest point, and when I needed it most, He stepped in to comfort me with His presence on that day. Over something as seemingly trivial as a break-up, He does care for me. He cares for all of us, as if each one of us was His only child. And then I remembered 1 Peter 5:7, which says "Cast all your cares upon Him, because He cares for you."

Colleen

"In the multitude of my anxieties within me, Your comforts delight my soul." Psalm 94:19

REASON # 15

HE EMPOWERS US

I gave my heart to Jesus up in Fairbanks Alaska in 1987. Two years later I went on a mission's trip to Taiwan, with a Chinese evangelist Nora Lam. She was going to be speaking in the city of Hualien. On the plane approaching the city she announced that there was a hurricane heading straight for it. So we all came in agreement and commanded the hurricane to turn – in Jesus name! When we got to the hotel all the hotel workers were telling us we were going to have to cancel the meeting – a hurricane is coming! We said, no, we prayed it away! They looked at us like we were off our rockers!!!

The next morning when we all came down for breakfast – they were looking at us funny! The hurricane did a 90° turn – and went out into the ocean, totally missing the island! That taught me that just like Jesus said, the works that He did, we would do also – and greater!

At the meetings that were held, Nora would preach in Chinese, and we Americans would make two lines face to face, and those who gave their heart to the Lord would walk between us, kind of like a gauntlet line, and we would pray for them quickly as they passed by. And then we would hand out Bibles. The one night when we were finished, I was talking to a lady from Oregon, when a Chinese woman came up to us pounding her fists on the side of her head! We thought, "Wow! This lady has a NASTY headache!" So we prayed against the headache pain, in the name of Jesus, and finished our prayer with "Thank You Jesus for healing our sister!" When we finished our prayer she started jumping up and down – going berserk! We didn't know what was wrong with her! People started running over to see what the problem was! We fearfully said, "We didn't do anything! All we did was pray for her headache! Honest! We didn't do anything to her!!" It turns out that she was deaf – and her ears popped open!

They had a booth in front of the stage full of deaf folks, with signers signing the message to them. Part of the message was Jesus saying "And these signs shall follow those who believe …. They shall lay their hands on the sick and they will recover!" So it was HER FAITH to get somebody who believed in the name of Jesus to lay hands on her! We were not in agreement while we were praying against what we thought was a headache. But as soon as we said "Thank you for healing our sister" – we were in agreement with her faith, and the miracle came!

Bill

"Most assuredly, I say to you, he who believes in Me, the works that I do he will do also; and greater works than these he will do, because I go to My Father." John 14:12

REASON # 16

HE NEVER GIVES
UP ON US

B ob and Patsy's testimony is of an ever faithful God. A God
 who is dependable... even when we are not. Everything He
  initiates He sees through to the end, including His relentless
pursuit for our hearts. God's pursuit of Patsy's heart began when
she was just 10 years old. Jesus made Himself very real to her and
she followed Him with child-like faith. Bob was twenty when he
met God and began to live for Him. Both enjoyed close
relationships with Jesus before they met. But, once married, they
began to drift away from their church and, ultimately, God.

Sometimes, we wander away from Christ so slowly, that one day
we wake up and find ourselves in a place we never expected –
distanced from God. Other times we walk away purposely,
believing we don't need Him. Either way, God never gives up on
His children. His very character is complete loyalty and devotion.
This is the message of Bob and Patsy's story...

After twenty years of marriage, without God as the center, Bob
and Patsy began to realize something was missing. What they
didn't see coming was that God was about to fill that enormous
emptiness in their heart. The gentle wooing of God's Spirit was at
work awakening them again to the relationship that laid dormant
for almost twenty years. The Holy Spirit began to melt Patsy's

hardened heart, and she found herself longing to be in God's presence again. She recalled the sweet fellowship of her church family, she longed to be with other believers. Unbeknownst to Patsy, God was also speaking to Bob's heart. At his place of work, Bob would pick up the "Our Daily Bread" devotionals he saw lying around, and would read them. God was definitely up to something!

Suddenly, one day Bob looked Patsy in the eyes and said, "We need to go back to church." Patsy was flabbergasted! Neither knew God had been working behind the scenes to bring them

both back into relationship with Him again. Today, Bob and Patsy are serving the Lord joyfully in their local church and can't imagine their life without God, or the fellowship of other believers. As Patsy puts it, "Now we get to serve God together. Hallelujah!"

Their story resembles that of the Prodigal Son in the Bible (Luke 15:11-32). Despite a father's love and devotion toward his son, the young man turns his back on his father and demands his inheritance, leaving home to pursue a life of indulgence. Eventually, he squanders all his money, loses his friends and longs to go back home. Everything the young man was searching for he had all along. He returned home broke and repentant, and didn't expect open arms when he returned home. He was ashamed of his behavior, but his father never turned his back on his son. It was clear that the only thing that mattered was that his son was home.

God's love is bigger than our ability to comprehend it. He calls us friends. And what Patsy was about to find out, was that this friendship included God's desire to fulfill her dreams. Before Patsy met Bob she dreamed of being an Airline Stewardess, to travel the world. However, after marrying and having children, her family was her first priority, so Patsy's dreams to travel were put on hold. While Patsy raised children, her sister – a successful business woman – was required to travel the country for work, and meet clients. You could imagine how excited Patsy was when her sister requested her assistance to accompany her on many business trips. She knew her sister could manage fine without her, but she was grateful that God chose to fulfill her dreams through her sister. God seems to know just how to work out the smallest of details in our lives, bringing us joy unspeakable! Patsy and Bob now see God even in the smallest of details in their lives, never taking His love for granted again.

Bob & Patsy

"If we are faithless, He remains faithful; He cannot deny Himself." 2 Timothy 2:13

REASON # 17

HE SETS US FREE

In Buffalo NY, and many cities across the country, there are healing ministries available. Their volunteers pray and intercede for the people who walk through their doors. They offer their services a few times a week and pray for people who are in need of physical and spiritual deliverance. They are trained in methods of prayer that address the root of bondage, and the breaking of strongholds and ties that we unknowingly make with the enemy when we believe his lies. What a blessing these people are to the church and community. If you are in need of prayer, I encourage you to find a local "Healing Rooms" ministry in your community. I've attended several sessions myself, and I can tell you, not only are you set free when you leave, but you realize that these people are genuinely concerned about you, and for your healing, so you can live a victorious life! Their services are free to the public and have one goal in mind, your complete healing! Body, soul, and spirit.

Their Pastor sent me a few examples of the kind of miracles God performs as they minister:

1. One of their staff members was diagnosed with double breast cancer. She went to three different doctors and all three came up with the same diagnosis. After receiving prayer, she submitted to surgery but as they operated the

doctors couldn't find anything. Again, they convinced her to have surgery once more insisting they had missed it. After prayer she submitted to surgery again. They repeated the surgery and once again found nothing!

2. A woman came to the healing rooms on her way to the hospital, scheduled for surgery. Her suitcase was in the car and she just stopped in for prayer. She got to the hospital, and had her surgery, but the doctors couldn't find anything!

3. A woman broke her shoulder bone, and after prayer the bones rejoined. This same person had a stroke and lost the use of her left side. After prayer she went into a coma for 4 days, and woke up with full use of her body with no paralysis! The doctors said she should have died.

4. Prayer was given on behalf of someone needing a kidney transplant. After the course of a year, and many promises from the hospital, discouragement began to set in. But one day after prayer someone just walked into the hospital to donate a kidney and it was a perfect match!

5. A woman in the hospital requested prayer for her Leukemia, and after prayer, was totally healed!

This is just a short list of the everyday healings these ministries see as they petition God to perform miracles in people's lives!

Pastor Don

"The Lord is near to all who call upon Him, to all who call upon Him in truth. He will fulfill the desire of those who fear Him; He also will hear their cry and save them. Psalm 145:18,19

REASON # 18

HE IS WITH US IN OUR STRUGGLES

When we don't conquer unhealthy habits, they often spiral out of control, into full-blown addictions. Smoking is one such habit. It may start as a stress reliever or what we view a "harmless" social habit. Then, boom! Before we know it, we're hooked. And, no matter how good our intentions or how often we try, we can't seem to quit. Dependency can happen to anyone and has many forms – drugs, alcohol, food, unhealthy relationships, etc... Dependency doesn't mean you are a bad person. It simply means you made a bad choice. But, praise God, He has the power to help us overcome our addictions and be set free!

Years of smoking had taken its toll on my body. For over ten years, I tried to quit multiple times but failed miserably. I knew God wanted me to stop but I just couldn't seem to, no matter how hard I tried. Finally, I tried the nicotine patch, thinking it was my answer. So, when that didn't work, I was devastated! I felt like a complete failure, as I realized cigarettes were literally consuming me. I wondered how other people could quit smoking when I couldn't. I felt utterly defeated! I was devastated and sorrowful because I had promised the Lord I would stop so many times... again... and again... and again!

Finally, I decided, "Enough is enough!" So, I cried out to God in anguished prayer. This time, I also asked my friends to support me in prayer. I was fiercely determined to be free of Nicotine, once and for all. I am overjoyed to tell you that God set me free instantly! Nothing is impossible for my God!!! You may be wondering why my attempts failed? It's because I was trying to do it in my own strength. Jesus heals our cravings and addictions, not us. He is the only one who can set us free because He alone is the Divine Healer. As the Bible says, "By His stripes we are healed" (Isaiah 53:5). Until I cried out in total surrender and gave it all to Jesus, my best efforts were all in vain. I was literally just "spinning my wheels" because there was no power in it.

When I humbled myself and surrendered it all to Jesus, He met me right where I was. As the loving Savior He is, He tenderly took my hand and led me out of the dark labyrinth of addiction and into His glorious light! I am so thankful for a God who knows exactly what His children need and delivers them. He delights in us and wants us healthy and free!

GG

"He brought me out into a spacious place; he rescued me because he delighted in me." Psalms 18:19

REASON # 19

HE MAKES ALL
THINGS NEW

During my early 20's, I suffered from severe clinical depression. I grew up not knowing God. I wasn't born into a Christian family, and I didn't meet my first Christian friend until I was 21, while at work. The depression continued to worsen until I couldn't work and was placed on disability. I thought, "My life is over!" My Christian friend stood beside me, visited me often, and encouraged me, telling me everything would be alright. I kept thinking, "How could she know?" I watched her walking in peace, love, and joy. I wanted that! So, I asked if I could attend church with her and her family (her husband and baby).

I felt better that day, the Sunday I attended church with them, but it didn't last. I sank deeper and deeper into depression and contemplated suicide. I tried counseling and saw a psychiatrist. I'd feel better... briefly. Then sink back into a deep, black abyss of depression again. I heard the Gospel message of Jesus, at my friend's church but I didn't think God wanted me, with all of my flaws. At my lowest point, I made a plan to overdose on prescription pills my psychiatrist prescribed me. I called poison control and told them my roommate was planning to overdose, naming the medication. They told me it would be lethal and I should call her psychiatrist stat! I thought, "Good! Now I will finally find the peace I've been longing for."

I waited for my roommate to go to work. Once she left, I overdosed! I thought I'd be dead when she returned home. But, to my surprise, I was still walking around my apartment when she arrived home. Eight hours later, she called an ambulance and they rushed me to ECMC. I was in a coma for three days. The doctors told my family, *if I lived*, I'd most likely have brain damage and need to be on dialysis for the rest of my life.

But God! He had a very real plan for my life. I awoke three days later from the coma. When I realized I hadn't died as planned, I knew only God could've saved my life. So, I surrendered my heart to Him. I told Him I didn't want my life, so I was giving it to Him to make something out of it. Immediately upon surrendering, God filled me with His peace. The peace I had been looking for.

A peace I had never known before… so real… so true. Best of all, He surrounded me with His love – a love I'd never been blessed with before. Then, He filled me with JOY! I was literally a different person! I can't describe what it's like to be filled with God's Holy Spirit, but I can tell you, it's life changing!

Just 5 days after being rushed to the hospital, I was released. I continued to attend church and be discipled. In just a few months, God blessed me with a new job, a car, and a new home. I was on my way… living life God's way. He had given me a second chance! I am now 60 years old and a new creation in Christ!!!

Anonymous

"Therefore, if anyone is in Christ, he is a new creation; old things have passed away; behold, all things have become new."
2 Corinthians 5:17

REASON # 20

HE TAKES CONTROL

One of the most helpless feelings we can ever experience is fear. Things just happen to us when we least expect it and the next thing you know we go into survival mode. That happened to me while behind the wheel of my GEO Tracker one late night. I was driving down a back road at high speed, and out of the corner of my eye I saw a deer who decided it was a good idea to run right out right in front of me as I was speeding by! With no time to hit the brakes, I could do nothing but continue full speed ahead and plow right into him.

I had never hit a deer before, but I've been told if you try to swerve and avoid hitting an animal, you may flip your car or even worse run into another vehicle and harm someone with you. I'm so glad I didn't have time to think because if I did I probably would have tried to avoid the collision and run off the road and flipped my little GEO Tracker. Because I plowed right into him, the deer didn't make it, and my car was totaled. I escaped uninjured, but I remember it took me a littles while to stop shaking after the accident.

This next short story I received resonates of divine intervention as she encountered some deer too…

I used to live off of River Road, in the Town of Tonawanda. Late one night as I was driving down a desolate road near the railroad tracks of my home, 4 deer decided to run right out in front of me, one after the other. The Holy Spirit immediately took over as I began braking and accelerating within seconds of each other. I seemed to dodge one deer, and the next one came into my path. I dodged that one, and again came another, braking and accelerating in between each animal, I managed to avoid all 4 deer! The only evidence of the incident was on the front passenger side where my headlight was cracked and the remnants of deer hair remained. I don't know how I did it, but I'm pretty sure Jesus took the wheel that night! I would consider that a miracle from the Lord God Almighty who cares for me!

When I read Anna's story, it made me smile. ☺

We can take for granted life's daily experiences, or we can turn our thoughts towards God and be reminded in those moments that someone is watching over us!

Anna Sorrento

"The angel of the Lord encamps all around those who fear Him, and delivers them." Psalm 34:7

REASON # 21

HE SAVES ME
FROM MYSELF

I grew up as a teenager in Buffalo NY back in the 60s, in a part of town that was RENOWNED for heavy drinkers. And to "be cool" you started drinking and drugging at a young age. I started when I was about 15.

Of course with any addiction, it starts out "just having fun", then after a while you're hooked! Alcoholism ran in my family, with both my grandfather's dying due to alcoholism before I was even born. And me, having a very competitive spirit, I had to out drink and get more stoned than any one of my friends!

I was smart enough to stay out of trouble. Although one time I blacked out at the wheel and ran into a church! Hitting the church shook me awake and the first thing that I could see in my mind's eye was my mom on her knees praying! All the police and paramedics said I should have been dead, BUT GOD!

Depression started setting in, with thoughts of suicide. To get away from my "people, places, and things" I ran away to Alaska – where I got even worse. The depression and self-loathing were so bad I couldn't talk to people. And the only job I could get was as a salesman – straight commission! I would drive around in my car and just cry, because I couldn't go into a customer's office and talk to them.

Drugs were much more available and I was at the point where I was actually planning my suicide. Just trying to decide whether I should slice my wrist, or drive my car off a cliff.

BUT GOD! I "just happened to find" a Gideon's New Testament with Psalms and Proverbs. The word of God LITERALLY saved my life! I would read and read and cry out to God! My job then transferred me up to Fairbanks from Anchorage. A guy I worked with invited me to come hear a guest speaker at his church one evening. After the speaker, one of the shyest guys in the church started talking to me, asking me if I knew Jesus. I sheepishly said yeah! But as I drove away I started thinking – "I know ABOUT Him, but I don't really KNOW Him!"

So I gave my heart to the Lord up in Fairbanks, and then my job transfer me back to Anchorage. I had been a drunk and a drug addict for about 15 years. If you've never been there it's hard to explain, but I HAD TO get drunk or stoned all the time!

What we used to do every payday at my job, which was every other week, a group of us would go to a Mexican restaurant and I would down five or six grandes – double margaritas – every Friday night! After I gave my heart to the Lord, when I was back down to Anchorage, the first payday we went to the same restaurant, I had one single margarita, then went to drinking iced tea! My manager, who was my drinking buddy, looked at me and yelled, "You can't do that Sullivan!! I know you better!!" The addiction was gone and I hadn't even realized it!

Later on I was invited out to lunch at a bar/restaurant that I used to hang out in. I never went there to eat, I didn't even know they had an entrance to the restaurant! When I walked in the bar, I felt totally out of place! And started thinking back "When was the last time I was in a bar?" It'd been about 6 or 8 months! I hadn't had a drink in six or eight months!!! The more I thought, I hadn't gotten stoned in over a year!!!! God totally delivered me – and I didn't even have to try!!

Bill

"Therefore if the Son makes you free, you shall be free indeed."
John 8:36

REASON # 22

HE WATCHES
OVER ME

There is one thing that every believer will do when faced with a crises... PRAY. We will proclaim God's promises over our lives and hold Him to His word. It is where our power lies and our victory is won. This next couple, has written about a time in their life when their faith in God meant everything, and their recovery hinged on speaking God's promises of healing. Their example teaches us to walk by Faith, and not by sight...

Bob and I had spent a great time in Florida during February and March, where we had rented a condo in Fort Myers. We had been doing this for the last few years, escaping the winters in Buffalo. We loved to spend time with our son Wayne, as his condo was across the street from us. On Easter Monday, April 9th, 2007 we started back to Buffalo. The sun was shining and it was a beautiful day. After driving for several hours, my husband didn't feel right and decided to get some sleep. I took over the driving, and about noon that day, I must have dozed off for a second. I tried to regain control of the car but could not, and we went off the 95 near Charleston, South Carolina. We landed in a brush of trees, bloody and crying out for help. A trauma nurse had been behind our car and she came to our aid. She applied pressure to my husband's forehead and probably saved his life as he was now losing a lot of blood.

We were cut out of the car and I was taken to the closest hospital. Bob was airlifted to the Medical University of South Carolina. While we were awaiting help, we were both conscious and Bob prayed. Later on, we were to learn that the trauma nurse in our car was crying out to the Lord on our behalf for the Lord to spare us. During this time I turned to the Word of God for comfort. I believe God's Word is true and that He accomplishes what He says. I quoted healing scriptures daily and tried to think positive thoughts each day. There was no room for negative thoughts even though the news was not always good. I believe that my husband's improvement each day, and what brought him through, was our faith in the Lord that we exercised - trusting in His power completely.

I was happy when I heard some of the hospital staff say that Bob came through because of the faith of the family.

The saying, "it's not hard to trust an unknown future to a known God" became a part of my conversation. Our children, and our grandchildren, as well as our sons-in-law were my support system. Our friends, neighbors, the firemen, our relatives and even the people we just met in the hospital were sent by God. Without these individuals, I don't know what I would have done. I pray for each and every one of them that God would bless them and take care of them because there is no way I can humanly repay everyone for what they did for my husband and myself at this time. God sent His Angels from everywhere to assist us until we could get on our feet. I believe the Lord was with us throughout this whole time. I pray God blesses each and every one beyond even what they could expect or even imagine.

Bob & Patricia Cummings

"Pray without ceasing."

1 Thessalonians 5:17

REASON # 23

HE INVITES US INTO
HIS KINGDOM

This next testimony is one of my favorite kind of testimony… it's one of a lost soul that has been given new life! We all start here when it comes to Jesus. This is a level playing field, and where we all begin our journey with God…

God has been so faithful to me. I was raised Catholic and this was always a part of me and I never walked away from church, or a faith in the God I knew (or thought I knew). But early in my marriage I struggled. After a huge disagreement with my husband. I left the house and just walked and walked. It was the end of December and snow covered the ground as I walked and talked. I was really talking to God. The specific thing I remember I said was, "Please show me what to do. I don't want to look to the left or to the right. Let me just look to You. You show me." I was a part of the Bishop's Committee (for young mothers) and we had a gathering at church to talk about why we believe what we believe. God showed up for me big time. We broke up in small groups, and in my group was Monica, and she spoke of living her life by the Bible. I was intrigued. When we went back into our large group, Monica boldly stood up and testified how God had changed her life. Everyone else was snickering – but I wasn't. I was drawn. When the meeting was over, I just stayed. It took a while, but I needed to talk to Monica. This was very unlike me to approach someone I didn't know. But there was no question what I needed to do. So I went to Monica and said "What is it about you?" I had to know and she began to tell me how the Lord changed her life. She needed a ride home, so as we drove together I listened to her retell what God had done for her. Through our conversation and some subsequent phone calls, she told me about watching the 700 Club, and also attending a prayer meeting at the Catholic Church. The Charismatic Renewal was within the Catholic Church. I started to go. On May 11th, 1975, I accepted Jesus as my personal Savior and have never looked back. When God comes into your life there's no doubt that something powerful has just happened! You are never the same when you meet God… He is good! Today, I attend the Tabernacle in Orchard Park. I feel God's presence every time I walk through those doors…

Today, get alone with God. Ask Him that all important question, "If You are real I need to know, and I need to know what that means to me personally." The Bible talks about turning from our sins, and asking Jesus into our hearts so that we can know His love. Let today be the first day of your new life with God!

Judi M.

"Give thanks to the LORD and proclaim His greatness.
Let the whole world know what He has done."
Psalm 105:1

REASON # 24

HE CARES

In our humanity, we often limit God in regard to miracles. We tend to assume God is only in the "big" healings, like serious or life-threatening illnesses and injuries. However, God is concerned about every aspect of our health. Yes, even a simple common cold. "Why would a God so big be interested in something so minor?" Because He is our Heavenly Father and, like any loving earthly parent, what hurts us hurts Him. I developed a very painful ear infection. I couldn't see a doctor because I had no money, not even a credit card. I was in so much pain. I didn't know what to do! Resting on the couch, I was channel surfing and came across a healing ministry on the television. As I continued to watch the program, the evangelist said, "Stand up and believe for your healing!" I believe God is our great physician, so I stood up and believed that He could do it. With all my heart and mind I believed God would be heal me. As we were praying, I felt a warm heat going through my ear. I knew I was being healed by the Lord instantly, and sure enough, there was no more pain! Dear Friend, our Heavenly Father is concerned with each and every part of your life, so do not limit Him. His love and compassions are immeasurable!   Gail B.

"Yes, I have loved you with an everlasting love." Jeremiah 31:3

REASON # 25

HE SINGS
OVER ME

Someone had recently said to me… "Mary, your breakthrough is going to be in your worship." I couldn't agree more. The power of worship has the potential to take you to the mountain top and push back the enemy at the same time! Those words have resonated in my spirit and have kept me focused when I find myself trying to do things in my own strength. I just refocus on worshiping God and there it is… my breakthrough!

This next testimony is all about worship too. It was the breakthrough in this women's life that freed her from bondage, false religion, and self-rejection…

A few years ago I had my daughters music teacher ask me a question…he said "Diane can I ask you a question and will you be completely honest with me?" I said, "Sure." He said, "I have never in all these years knew anyone that came to the Lord from watching someone dance. Can you seriously tell me that you know someone that was saved through seeing dance?" I said, "Actually yes… me."

I had been brought up in a home where there was no dance, no TV, no radio, no newspaper…basically nothing "of the world" was allowed in the house. Dance definitely wasn't even a thought because there was no way that would be allowed. But, one of my friends took dance lessons, and the few times I was allowed to go to her house she'd show me her dances. That was my first exposure to dance and something about this movement tugged at my heart; I knew my parents considered it "sin" but I was moved and inspired by the way it made me feel. Fast forward some years...I was invited to see "The Bride" at a church. A church! Well that's what got me into a church...some friends told me they were going to this show and invited me to go. I was a mess at the time of this invite...mainly suicidal because of my past. During this performance there was dancing and one of the dancers caught my eye...the way she expressed herself...her facial expressions...her physical expression...it was like she was expressing her love relationship with this Jesus I did not know...I only knew a God that had all these rules for me to follow or I was going to go to hell...and not dancing was one of those rules and yet...yet deep inside something told me that's what I was called to do...that is where my journey of dance began. Dance became the voice I didn't have...in being a woman, and freeing me from the pain of my past. This is me... free at last, by the grace of God!

When I shared this story with that teacher he appeared a bit shocked and didn't know what to say. It became my testimony... a testimony, His testimony...through dance I have learned to make that private cry public... praying that God uses me to continually say yes...to express His amazing unconditional love. Someone may be exactly where I was many years ago, and I pray my dance before the King will draw them to the only one that saves...Jesus!!

Diane

"The LORD your God is in your midst.
The Mighty One, will save; He will rejoice over you with gladness, He will quiet *you* with His love, He will rejoice over you with singing." Zephaniah 3:17

REASON # 26

HE CALLS ME
FRIEND

I believe that my testimony began way back in about 1967. I have memories of walking to the local Catholic Church as a 6 year old with my siblings. I'm so thankful for a Catholic mother who thought it was important enough to send us off to church. I don't remember any resistance, just, this is what you do. So growing up, I came to the conclusion that there is a God. I had no reason to dispute it, though I surely wasn't looking for Him. Looking back now, I see it really didn't do me any good because I only knew to live for myself and maybe even the devil.

So as one can imagine, my life easily ran out of control by the time I was 27. After my 3rd DWI, along with a failed relationship, I was at the point of giving up on life. I knew I didn't want to go through that DWI process again. So I spent the last of my cash at the bar, which was right below my apartment, and was figuring on getting a gun the next day and checking out.

Now as funny as this may sound, the thought that deterred me was - if there is an eternity, my mom would nag me for all eternity for killing myself. So I opted to just tough it out. I knew the party life was over for me. Well, that put me in such a depressed state that I didn't eat for 3 days. I worked, and took care of court matters, but my life was over. Then, on the 4th day at work, someone said something funny, and I began to laugh. Then turning around back to my machine, I remember a voice saying, "What are you laughing at, your life is over." And as I usually just accept things as they are, I agreed and said, "oh yeah that's right." At that moment, I said in my heart, "oh God, if only You could help me?" You see, I had made my bed and now I had to sleep in it.

But God had another plan. At that very moment, such a heavy cloud of depression lifted right off me. That was absolutely amazing. Tears of joy began to roll down my face. Not so much about the depression lifting, but the realization that God could be that close. I had no idea. He filled that Jesus shaped hole that was in my heart and I have not desired to fill it with anything else ever since. I have learned to walk with God, to the best of my ability anyway, and can attest that I've been sober and drug free for the last 29 years.

*****

This testimony is a great example of how God changes us completely! Have you ever listened to someone tell their personal journey, and as you're listening your jaw is dropping? Well, mine is dropping right now. Not because of the curveballs life will throw at us, but because I only know this man on the other side of these events and he is such an exuberant, fun loving, and carefree person. He is the poster child for joy. His love for God, His servant's heart, and the effortless knack to make you laugh and smile is the best way I can describe him. It's been said that the enemy of our soul only knows one way to operate, and that is to lie to us. Well, I'm so glad this man chose not to believe Satan's lies anymore. Our Creator knows the beginning from the end of our story… the real story He has written for our lives. God gives us beauty for ashes, and joy for mourning. He meets us right where we're at and invites us to join in His eternal celebration. The never-ending joy, peace, love, and truth about who we are, who He is, and all He has instore for us. If you find yourself alone, confused, and afraid, don't wait another moment to ask Jesus to open your eyes and to reveal to you just how much He loves you. He's waiting for you to call on Him… that's all it takes.

Bob

"For God did not send His Son into the world to condemn the world, but that the world through Him might be saved." John 3:17

REASON # 27

HE HAS A PLAN
FOR ME

I have an identical twin brother who accepted Jesus as his Savior in 1989. His life was totally different and I knew something had changed in him. I was curious as to what brought my brother to this decision. He said that he wanted to know why he was created and he asked Jesus to come into his heart, pleading the blood of Jesus over himself, and then the next thing he knew the Holy Spirit came into his room and baptized him.

When he invited me to a Christian service, I decided to go. It didn't take long before the Holy Spirit began to touch me as well. I began to feel my heart change. I started to pray and wanted the same thing my brother had. After about a year in May 1990 I was laying on my bed. It was a quiet May night and my window was wide open and there was not even a breeze. I continued to say my prayers, for all my aunts and uncles that had passed before me, saying the "Our Father." And after this, I remember asking Jesus to come into my heart. I told Him I wanted to know him; I wanted to know why He created me. All of a sudden a great wind came through my window that blew the curtains to the ceiling. It sounded like a locomotive came into my room, the whole atmosphere changed and God's presence was everywhere. I began to weep and cry and couldn't move. I felt a fire and a warmth come over my entire body. It was like all the stress, and all this pain, and hurting instantly left my body, it was like I felt Jesus hugging me. I asked Him to give me a heart for the youth, so that I could teach a generation the things that I went through so they didn't have to go through it like I did. I also asked God to help me be a good father to my son Eddie who was five years old, and a good husband. The next morning when I woke up, the sun was shining and it was a beautiful day. I had never felt this way ever in my life. It was the greatest feeling in the world! I went down to the Bible Society and bought two cases of Bibles and went up and down my street telling every neighbor what happened to me. I also went to a couple of my ex-drug dealers and gave them a Bible and told them that I got born-again and that Jesus came into my heart and that they could have that also. It's hard to explain what happens to a person when they meet God, but I can tell you this... you are never the same!

Eddie

"Now then, we are ambassadors for Christ, as though God were pleading through us: we implore you on Christ's behalf, be reconciled to God." 2 Corinthians 5:20

REASON # 28

HE SAVES THE
NATIONS

My name is Hemamalini Sakthivel. I want to share how the Lord Jesus has been good to me and my family and the countless miracles He performed for us. I will share some of the most important ones for His glory, and to have faith for your situations.

Firstly my family and I were translated from the kingdom of darkness to the marvelous Kingdom of HIS Son (light). I belong to a very religious, ardent and orthodox Hindu family. I was taught by my parents and grandparents to worship idols, recite scriptures called slogams and perform rituals to please and fear God. My mom had given her heart to the Lord Jesus while in elementary School. Due to her circumstances and having no opportunity to know more about the Lord, she slowly began following her family's Hindu traditions. However the Lord never forget her commitment and had a plan to seek her once again through me, her daughter.

Since Christian Schools in my Country (India) had a reputation of having good academics, and moral values, many parents enroll their kids in these Schools. I too was enrolled in one called C.S.I. Bain Matriculation and Higher Secondary School in Chennai, Tamil Nadu. All students irrespective of their faith, were given opportunity to sing songs to worship and participated in Hall prayer every morning and evening. That prayer has rescued me from predators while walking home from school and saved me from accidents.

While studying in 8th grade, I became friends with Rachel, a Christian Indian girl. During the middle of the school year, her father passed away. My friend exhibited such peace, calmness and faith in her God Jesus during the most sorrowful time of her life. Having seen how Hindus expressed their tears, sadness and uncertainty about after life, following the loss of a family member, was different from the confident hope of my friend in seeing her dad in eternity with her God Jesus.

My friend's testimony and friendship made me seek the true Loving, Living Savior who she believed was going to take the place of her father in caring for her mom and 3 siblings.

I had an ambition to become a medical doctor. So I worked very diligently to secure good grades in school. Unfortunately a sinus infection that wouldn't go away made me lose several classes. Though I fared quite good in my finals, due to the competitive nature in getting admission to Medical School, I couldn't get a spot that year. I was heart-broken and disappointed and so was my mom.

Before my results came, I had been to a prayer meeting at my friend Rachel's home. Here, one minister of God prophesied (I didn't know what prophesy meant at the time) that God would give me admission into Medical School. Though the disappointment of not getting what I desired was there, the word of the Lord given to me was giving me hope. The Lord who saw my mom and my tears and my faith in Him, opened a new door in one year for my dream of studying in Medical School.

With new found faith in the Lord Jesus, I began my journey as a medical student. Not knowing the fundamentals of the Christian faith or real meaning of salvation, I faced a hard time to counter attack the things of the enemy against me. Nevertheless The Lord delivered me from every evil, brought about by my own ignorance and the witchcraft done by some mean people who did not like the Lord's blessing on my life. During this trial season, I submitted to water baptism as a sign to the devil that I totally surrendered my life to the King of Kings.

My parents did not object to me following the Lord Jesus, but as a young female from Hinduism, I had restrictions from going to Church every Sunday. However my mom and me went to a ministry called Jesus Calls prayer tower. Here we received prayers from the prayer warriors and God's servant uncle D.G.S. Dhinakaran and bro. Paul Dhinakaran. This ministry specifically meets the needs of people like me who follow Christ amidst persecution.

With God's help I completed Medical School and residency and became a physician. In India, families look for the bride or bridegroom for their children (arranged marriage). I did not know even to pray for my parents or my brother's salvation at that time. The only thing I knew is that my father would never come to Jesus if I insisted on marrying a Christian.

So I fasted and waited patiently for the Lord to choose a bridegroom from my own Hindu caste and community. The Lord impressed in my heart that He would show me the man He has chosen for my life. He said the first man who comes to see you at your home would be the person I have kept for you. True to that promise, my husband Sakthi was the only man who came and saw me at my home with his family to seek my hand in marriage.

My husband was working in California and after my wedding, I came to the United States. Coming to the USA was also one of my life-long dreams and the Lord fulfilled it too. After knowing my faith in the Lord Jesus, my husband was upset that I did not tell him that before my wedding. As my husband believed in covenant, he never abandoned me. The Lord also helped me to be a good witness by submitting to my husband in things other than my faith according to 1 Peter 3:1, 2. God gave favor in my husband's eyes.

I was believing for a Christian friend who should also have met Jesus from a Hindu background. It was next to impossible as I was new to the US and didn't drive at that time. The apartment we rented had only 12 condos. But God had already kept my friend Anu Girdhar a Hindu convert and her family in Apt 11. So we both met in a divine way at the laundry room. Her friendship and fellowship not only helped me spiritually but their love, prayers and visits blessed my husband and me.

Within 2 years into my marriage, my husband had a divine encounter in the night when he saw a shining bright light and a hand that placed a cross on his forehead. I was never able to witness or share my testimony to my husband. But God intervened in a supernatural way and there were a few subsequent incidences, like going with the Girdhar's to an Easter Service at Jubilee Christian Center in San Jose. Being a religious Hindu himself, my husband had been seeking God and he felt the presence of God, (Holy Spirit) at the Church Worship. He went forward to the altar and gave His life to the Lord Jesus that Easter in 1999. Since then He began a faith journey himself, running ahead of me, standing for the Lord amidst persecution from family members. He was filled with the Holy Spirit, and went witnessing for Christ at his office, down-town places, and even preached the Gospel in Africa and ministered to me and several others in the US and India.

A few other miracles I would like to mention here are, I was barren for 5 years and the Lord healed me completely from polycystic ovaries and enabled me to become a mom of two kids now 14 and 12 years old. The greatest miracle of all, my father (who now is with Jesus), my mom, mother-in-law and my brother became Christians. I also encountered several demonic oppositions and faced very difficult times in my life, but through it all the Lord Jesus has kept me, healed me, delivered me and set me free. I am a living testimony to the glory of Jesus my Lord and Savior. I am a living witness sharing God's love to many people and wanting them to taste and see that the Lord is good.

Hema S.

"Oh, taste and see that the LORD is good;
Blessed is the man who trusts in Him!" Psalm 34:8

REASON # 29

HE DOES WHAT
DOCTORS CAN'T

I was young in 1980, not yet 30, when I had my first exam with my new physician, Dr. Lonnie Walter. While listening to my heart, he detected something with his stethoscope, which he told me sounded like Mitral Valve Prolapse. Mitral Valve Prolapse is a condition in which a floppy mitral heart valve doesn't close completely, allowing some of the blood to flow backwards. To confirm his diagnosis, Dr. Walter ordered an EKG. The EKG confirmed the diagnosis.

During the next 20 years, I would occasionally feel my heart race briefly, even while completely at rest. I never felt any pain or sickness, only this occasional racing. During this time, I took antibiotics prior to visiting the dentist because any bacteria which might get into my bloodstream could cause a big problem if it got caught in that floppy valve. There were unpleasant side-effects to the large doses of antibiotics, but it was usually only twice per year, so learned to live with it. But I never stopped believing for my healing! Whenever someone would pray for hearts or share a word of knowledge concerning heart issues, I would raise my hand and receive it for myself. Oh, how I longed to see God's miraculous power in my life!

Eventually, the dosage of antibiotics lessened. Then, one day, my dentist told me some people with Mitral Valve Prolapse no longer needed to take antibiotics at all. He told me to consult my primary physician to see if I might be one of those people. By then, the echocardiogram had been developed, so we made an appointment.

About a week after my Echocardiogram, I received a phone call, and heard these words... "There is absolutely nothing wrong with your heart." I couldn't believe my ears! How could that be? God had healed my heart! Hallelujah! I've heard when people get healed they will feel heat, electricity, or some other physical sensation indicating that God is at work doing something. I didn't feel anything, unless the healing came when I was asleep or otherwise unaware of what was happening. So, I don't know exactly when but I know Jesus healed me!

I knew I had been healed! Yet, I also knew there were others who would doubt my story. So I made one more phone call, to a friend who was a nurse in cardiac research at that time. I told her what happened and asked her if mitral valve prolapse ever goes away on its own. She said it doesn't. Her words sealed the confirmation. My healing definitely happened and it was a *divine miracle* from God!

Jan Grek

"I will praise You, for I am fearfully and wonderfully made:
Marvelous are Your works, and that my soul knows very well."
Psalm 139:14

REASON # 30

HE HAS KNOWN ME FROM A CHILD

When I was just 7 years old I had severe eczema. My mother prayed for my healing every day. One night, the Eczema flared up so badly and I was in so much pain, my mother prayed through her tears. The next morning, while in the bathroom, I looked down at my feet and, and to my amazement and joy, I was totally healed! I got so excited I kept calling, "Mommy! Mommy! Mommy! Jesus healed me!!!" My faith began as a little child... because you can't deny it when you've been touched by God! But He had more in store for me...

A few years ago, I went to a new doctor. She checked my thyroid and found a nodule. Immediately, I was sent for a sonogram. The Doctor who read my report said, because of how vascular it was, there was a 95% it was cancer. A week later, I had a biopsy. They said it would take 10 days for the results. I continued to pray and had many people agreeing with me in prayer. One day, while I was praying, the Lord told me, "Do not pray about the cancer. Just pray about your thyroid." Well, the very next day my doctor called and said I was *cancer-free!* Hallelujah!!! God came through for me again!

And God wasn't done with me yet... In 2012, I was diagnosed with precancerous cells on my cervix, along with other female health concerns. Again, I took it to the Lord and had women praying for me, concerning the situation. In the process, I would pray and wait for my next appointment. Six months later, I had more tests done and the doctors told me I was fine! All pre-cancerous cells were gone!!! God has been faithful to me since a child, and I know He isn't finished with me yet!!

Maria Elizabeth

"Oh, satisfy us early with Your mercy, that we may rejoice and be glad all our days!" Psalm 90:14

REASON # 31

HE TEACHES US
TO FORGIVE

I was only 25 years old, and we already had three children. It was then when I received a call from my mother that I had better try to come home because in a drunken brawl my youngest brother Terry, who was two weeks away from his 21st birthday and two weeks away from the birth of his first son, was in the hospital in serious condition. Terry had a disagreement with his neighbor and friend over a television set. He had gone next door and had been drinking. A fight broke out between Terry and his friend and when Terry began to leave the yard, the friend pulled out a gun and shot him.

I took the first bus back to Indianapolis to see my brother. I walked into the hospital room to see him with his leg up and in a lot of pain. He had just gotten out of surgery and for the most part seemed like he was going to make it. He was very angry, of course, with the man who shot him and strongly expressed how he wanted to get out of there and kill him. Like an older sister, I began to tell him how much his wife and new baby needed him. I talked to him about the Lord and all the emotional healing that had taken place in my life. Because I loved my brother so much, I wanted to pray with him like we did when we were kids growing up. I also asked him to re-dedicate his life to the Lord Jesus and to ask God to touch his heart and forgive the young man who shot him; to acknowledge that the influence of alcohol was mostly to blame. I asked him to forgive this man and the Lord would forgive all of his sins if he were to ask. Immediately, the sweet spirit of the Lord entered that hospital room and my precious little brother, once again, (this time all grown up) gave his heart and anger to the Lord.

Well, after a bit, I kissed him goodbye, told him I would see him the next day and went to my mother's house to spend the night. At about 1 or 2 a.m. we received an alarming phone call from the hospital informing us that a blood clot had traveled from the gun shot into his heart and that my precious brother, who, just a few short hours before had received Christ, was in a coma and not expected to live. We all got dressed and rushed back to the hospital. I watched as my mom and dad clung to each other. I watched their pain; both of them helpless in this situation, and once again a faith and peace rose up in me as I asked them to pray with me for the Lord to touch him.

Connie, his young wife and mother-to-be could barely be consoled. We were concerned that she might have the child early. My sisters and other brother were broken hearted and scared. I went to the hospital chapel to bargain with the Lord of my life on behalf of my brother Terry. It seemed like hours (I am sure it was not that long) as I heard the staff saying words like, "hopeless" and "brain dead." This time I went into the chapel and this was my prayer:

"Lord, you are saying no more deals." Jesus loved my brother even more than I did. At first, I tried to make a deal, that if he would save my brother's life, I would serve the Lord for the rest of mine. This time, I said, "Lord, Your will be done, and I will serve

You anyway and anywhere You would have me serve," and I prayed for my family and the opportunity for all of them to accept Him and His plan of salvation for their lives.

I went back to Terry's room and my mother and father could barely speak. They were devastated. It was so hard to see him hooked up to the life support, knowing they needed to decide that if he was brain dead, they would pull the plug. The next few days were blank. My husband came and helped all of us make it through; that man of steel, and velvet. The Lord knew what I would need, but the test of my faith was yet to come. Micah 6:8 asks the question: *"What does the Lord require of you; but to do justly, to love mercy, and to walk humbly with your God?"*

We made arrangements for the funeral. Needless to say, we were all emotionally devastated. For the first time, I had an opportunity to keep my promise. I stood by my brother's casket and told all who would listen how I knew he was with Jesus and that my brother had forgiven the man who shot him. Little did I know I was going to have to walk that walk and not just talk the talk, because who showed up at the funeral, but the broken young man who had shot our brother. He begged us to forgive him, but only God comes at times like these when, we, ourselves in the flesh, seem like we cannot find the love and mercy to humble ourselves and let His Holy Spirit take over and let His power, through us, forgive others who have hurt us beyond words or comprehension, He empowers us to choose His way and not the way of the world. *"What does the Lord require of you, to love mercy and forgive as He has forgiven us?"*

That day I watched as the enemy intended for more destruction to our family, a peace that surpasses all understanding, Terry was with the Lover of his soul, mine and yours. Jesus gives us what we need to make it through life's tragedies if we will choose to let Him. My brother did not die in vain. He did not die unsaved, and neither did his friends, wife or son, years later, long after my brother had passed away. The Lord made a way for me, if only for a short time. I was able to see my nephew, re-tell him the story of how his daddy forgave the man who shot him and offered him the opportunity to receive Christ. Therefore, when my nephew leaves this earth, he will see Jesus and the earthly father he never knew. Only the Lord Jesus makes a way where there seems to be no way.

DeeDee

"What does the Lord require of you; but to do justly, to love mercy, and to walk humbly with your God." Micah 6:8

REASON # 32

HE LEADS ME TO
TRUTH

This next submitted testimony caught me off guard. Honestly, I wasn't quite sure where it was going. But I will confess that it could now be one of my all-time favorites. Not because it unfolds a mind-blowing healing of miraculous proportions, no, it does more than that. It exposes a very real, very powerful, very dangerous deception… I am grateful for the candidness of this writer. And what may at first seem like a minuscule problem in this story, escalades to monumental proportions. She walks us through the psyche of the human mind, its vulnerability, and its potential to be a sitting duck for enemy attack... I believe this testimony will hit home to almost every one of us. I'm so glad when I get submissions that not only speak of God's ability to heal our physical bodies, but also our emotional and psychological struggles that need healing as well…

The basic story is this, I woke up, stubbed and broke my baby toe, prayed, and fell back to sleep. As morning appeared I did my best to hobble around getting ready for my day. I came to the first difficulty, finding a shoe that I could wear and walk in without pain. I now realized the intensity of the pain in this tiny member. That one little toe was really getting in my way. Why do we have baby toes anyway?!! I began to feel sorry for myself and went down a spiral of defeat, weakness, and feeling alone in my struggle. I felt a lack in ability, strength, and somehow let this little thing become too huge. I contacted my husband in hopes he would be stopping back home before going to our planned meeting tonight. I didn't get a response and I began waiting. Then I noticed he had left my vehicle parked across the street as he needed to access his own vehicle to leave early that morning. The whole thing went from a hurt toe to a hurt soul enjoying a pity party that rose up from my frustrations and grew when I finally heard back that he was almost to our meeting place and I would need to drive myself. Now I felt left alone and needed to decide: was I going to stay home or hobble across the street, and get in my car?

It is funny to me, as an afterthought, how this little toe incident grew in my mind, how frustration expanded into full blown anger at my husband who was not there, who had no idea about the incidents of the morning, but who was doing exactly as we had discussed the day before. Now my toe, the dog's food dish, the car being across the street, the difficulty walking in my shoe, having to drive and go to the meeting alone all began to swirl around me in a storm that existed only inside my head. I limped to the car and began my drive. Fighting back tears, the prayer I prayed was born from God's Spirit: *Lord, please help me forgive my husband, I would forgive anyone else, I don't know why I'm so mad at him, he wasn't even here, he didn't do anything wrong, there is no reason for me to be angry.* I heard in my heart, BE QUICK to forgive. Don't give the enemy a foothold.

I was on my way to what could be an awesome prayer meeting or a horrible scene of withdrawing in anger toward my husband who had done nothing wrong. I chose forgiveness. I don't even know if the word makes sense in this situation as there was nothing to forgive. Yet I spoke it to my listening ears that *I choose to forgive, that I love my husband and know he didn't park my car across the street to cause me trouble, he had no idea I would be injured.* I finished my prayer, wiped my tears, but I was still in pain. I arrived at my destination, found my way to the meeting and was warmly welcomed by some greeters. The love began to work on my raw emotions. As I headed toward the meeting door, I received another beautiful greeting from two friends. There I honestly admitted my painful situation and how it had affected my emotions in such a strong way. Before I stepped into that room, we prayed. The warrior prayers of fellow believers became a warm blanket of love and truth resting on tired shoulders, covering over the lies the enemy had tried to use as weapons against me, against my marriage, and even against this prayer meeting.

Had I walked in with my soul in disarray, the enemy would have entered as well. They spoke truth over me, stood me back up on my feet, dusted me off, and love came in like a flood over the enemy's strategy. I was physically hurting, my pain was real, my ability to walk normally was impaired and yes, I physically arrived alone, those facts were my reality. The enemy deceptively twisted the facts of the physical into an emotional mess of feeling weak, alone, hurt, and helpless...or WAHH! Can you hear the tears of self-pity crying out like a baby? But God... He was with me. Truth-He was there and He was my strength to keep me moving forward, to keep the dialogue real and the prayers prayed. He gave me grace to pray for healing and forgiveness and fight for the unity of my marriage. Truth-My reality at the time needed an act of forgiving my innocent husband. It wasn't until later that God sorted it all out and showed me the deception of the enemy at work and his scheme to divide us, to create conflict, to keep me home, or to unknowingly bring a wrong attitude to a prayer gathering. He put two prayer warriors in my direct path to meet me and pray so I could walk in from a new refreshed place of His strength, Kingdom community, healing, and overcoming. Truth.

We need to carefully guard our hearts from the deception of the enemy. He doesn't usually come to us in obvious ways to trip us up. He twists the facts and attacks at the soul level. But God is our defender, He speaks truth, He gives us the strength to press on and press through. There was a time I would have been defeated and not shown up- stayed home and isolated with the lies being dished out. God takes us from glory to glory and each situation is different, but it is an experiential process of walking out our faith that makes it real and puts muscles to the promises of His finished work in all of our lives.

So the last part of the testimony is that my husband, the innocent "almost victim" in this incident, and I were able to laugh with friends as we relayed the craziness of this particular day. We were able to share how God kept me all the way through it, kept my husband free from being "blamed", & kept our marriage united. Ironically the theme of the prayer meeting that day was, UNITY! We did not know this prior to our arrival at the meeting! Plus, the strategy to quickly forgive has been a continued helpful piece of advice, something I keep in my heart, a love note from God.

In Love

"And don't sin by letting anger control you. Don't let the sun go down while you are still angry, for anger gives a foothold to the devil" Ephesians 4:26,27

REASON # 33

HE MAKES ALL THINGS NEW

I remember the morning when I woke up and I was so very, very sick. Within a few short days I realized I was carrying baby number 6. I was so excited, but that soon wore off because the reality was that my husband was unemployed, and we had no insurance, and my fifth child was still in a crib in my bedroom. I wondered at that point if we could hang cribs from the ceiling!

We looked into putting an addition on our house but the funding just wasn't there. We barely had $100 a week to take care of all of us. There was no government assistance available, unless we were willing to put a lien against our house. The Lord said we were children of His, and not of the state, so I kept my eyes on Him… my provider. I remembered the scripture verse that said, "Children are a gift from the Lord, and the fruit of the womb is His reward… I knew He would provide for us.

At that time, a friend blessed me with an invitation to a conference. The worship was out of this world. I knelt down and put my head on the chair, and I began to weep. Honestly, I was not a crier. Immediately on the chair sat Jesus and I was in the throne room and my head was on His lap. He began to stroke my hair. I could feel His touch like nothing I've ever felt before. I could hear Him say" it will be okay, it will be okay." I wish I could live in that place today. As I stood, I sensed that all things were going to be NEW. And as I left the conference the speaker gave me a hug and said "God has something NEW for you."

When I arrived home I'm sure I was glowing, and I said to my husband, "we need to start the NEW addition." He was flabbergasted because I told him before, "don't even begin to dig a hole! How will we ever sell a house with a big hole, it will end up being a handyman special." I told him, "Where would we go if we had no finances to get a new mortgage and move." But now we were in a NEW day. A NEW Hope…

Within a few short months, with the help of all of our friends who just happened to be electricians, roofers, neighbors, and church people, we had our NEW two-story 20 x 12 addition. Bedrooms, closets, a parlor entrance, and a hall....ALL PAID FOR...PIECE BY PIECE... no laborer paid! All complete in time to welcome a brand

NEW life into this world - my beautiful baby boy. He was so

healthy and born at the Doctor's house to avoid hospital bills. God provided in every single way. And when the construction was done my husband received a NEW job. It paid 4 times over the other job. And through that encounter... of meeting God in the throne-room we have never had another financial need in our household.

Gail McCrory

"Then He who sat on the throne said, Behold, I make all things NEW." Revelations 21:5

Sometimes, we don't understand why God allows bad things to happen to good people. I have found this to be most true when loving people fall ill with terminal illness. We don't understand why God would allow such Godly people to suffer so much. Such was the case with one Sister-in-the-Lord, Alma Bemis, who selflessly dedicated her entire life to her own family, as well as her church family. She was a sweet, loving soul, always caring for and encouraging others, never expecting anything in return. Her greatest joy was found in serving the Lord by caring for others. That was her Calling from God…

Months after Alma was diagnosed with Cancer, she was seated in front of me in the church Prayer Tower. I wanted to tell her how great she looked, but God had another word. I asked God what He wanted me to tell her and He replied, "Tell her that she will help many receive their miracle, when her miracle is complete." So I did, I told her exactly what God wanted me to say. I expected her to be healed and to live.

My faith was tested deeply when Alma passed away. I couldn't understand why God would have me tell her that she would help many receive their miracle, when she received hers, if He didn't intend to heal her here on earth. After all, how could she touch many lives if she was no longer here to do so? But later, I was to find out through a conversation with her daughter-in-law, that Alma did, indeed, receive her miracle. She said her doctors only gave Alma 6 months to live but she lived another 6 years! During that time, she wrote two books, which encouraged many people. The years God gave her were her miracle. In this journey she placed her trust in God, and He gave her courage for each day. Her gift was the gift to encourage other people, especially through her pain. And like Job, her trust and love for God never wavered. This was her trophy… she finished the race strong.

I was stunned! I had no idea the words God chose to speak to Alma that day, through me, would be so prophetic. I didn't understand it at the time, but God knew Alma's destiny. I am thankful for the words He gave me, and I am thankful for the years He gave Alma.

Lord, I repent of the times I've questioned you. The times I thought I knew what was best and failed to hear you or purposely ignored You. May I always be slow to question and quick to listen to Your voice and do Your will. For You alone know what is truly best… always…and in all ways…because Your will is perfect.

Jean

"For the eyes of the Lord run to and fro throughout the whole earth, to show Himself strong on behalf of those whose heart is loyal to Him." 2 Chronicles 16:9

REASON # 35

HE GIVES ME A
VOICE

I was born in a small town in northern Minnesota – number 3 of 4 kids in a pretty ordinary basic dysfunctional home with a quietly angry WW II father and sweet but innocent mother. My first memory of God in my life was 3 years old at my great grandmother's funeral. I found myself looking down at this petite lady in the casket from my father's arms just as the audience sang the classic hymn "When the Role is Called Up Yonder I'll be There". Considering the vague title of the song I am still surprised that instantly I had a knowing of the reality of an eternity, and an overwhelming need to get there. Later in my Christian life I found a verse to substantiate my first experience with my eternal creator – Eccl. 3:11 "God has written eternity in the heart of man".

One summer at Bible Camp I had my next encounter with Christ. After a sermon about His saving grace I had a convicting lump in my throat that threatened to choke me so I went forward to accept Christ- get some relief. But my youthful mind – and no reinforcement from home - I misunderstood the message. I came home fully prepared to live sinless. After counting 10 behavioral sins on my fingers in 2 weeks, sitting on an old swing set and feeling bad, I apologized to Jesus and told him 'I could not live for Him', got up and walked away. But He never walked away from me.

My brother was a negative and predatory influence in my life, which deeply affected my esteem and encouraged me to second guess my worth. My father was emotionally unavailable and my mother leaned into me for emotional support early in my teens, so by the time I was 14 I decided that I could not trust their decision making and secured for myself a huge dose of mistrust and self-reliance.

I aggressively pursued the arts in high school. I loved dance so I studied dance and theater for several years. I rebelled against my parent's strict church attendance policy. I had aspirations in life that were not affirmed by them and I didn't care. 'Over achiever' was the working title for my totally self-involved destination.

As family dynamic declined further I was pretty restless, disappointed at 18, and ready to graduate from HS, my sister comes home as a radical Jesus follower. I fought it for several months.

Since I had gotten off the swing set my heart had hardened and my determination to become something sent me toward that gift I found in dance and theater. This was my on ramp to a fulfilled life; medicating my broken soul. When Jesus came back on the scene He was just in the way of my determined self-idolizing dream.

It took a while but I finally had another heart to heart with Jesus and told Him frankly that I didn't want Him. Then I mustered up my strength from somewhere (probably because I was fully aware of what eternity without Him would be) and asked him to "change my heart" I think my exact words were, "God, You got to make me want You".

Six month later I did, desperately want Him and committed my life to Christ. This time with full understanding of the transformation out of sin nature, reminding me that He started chasing me at 3 by my great grandmother's casket. Oh my…'how I was loved'. I realized it for the first time in my life. I found someone with a devoted nature whom I could trust. He had actually given His life to secure mine.

Two summers later I read "God's Smuggler" by a Dutch believer called Brother Andrew. He was a Bible smuggler during the height of Communist oppression in East Europe. After I finished it I was so deeply moved I could not loose it from my hands, literally 'could not put it down'. I still can't completely explain. This was another moment with God and I came to know, in just a few moments and with solid certainty, that I was supposed to do missions in oppressed nations. Here comes the call on my life but I did not have a clue how?

I had got into in the dental field for several years needing to sustain myself not knowing how I was going to make a missions call happen. I attended a Bible Study at a place called Miracle House and received what they called the Baptism in the Holy Spirit. I had never heard of it before. I was prayed for and one amazing result was an insatiable hunger for the Word, uncommon confidence and an assurance I really could do something for GOD. It really could happen. It felt other worldly.

I moved to Minneapolis and met the Peters family who owned and ran Camp Zion – a suburban Bible camp program that became a youth driven church and I got involved as a counselor and staff.

I lived and worked there for 4 years, involved in missions and music, attended North Central University ... getting a degree in Missions Education/Bible.

All the while God was deepening my heart for missions along with my friends Gary Krueger, and Jim and Debbie Peters. In 1981 we finally hatched a brave plan to leave on the road and pursue a call we all felt we had – Global Evangelism through music.

We named ourselves GTM. Left St. Paul, MN with a homemade trailer, a borrowed van, a loaned sound system, a $200 donation from a friend and 10 concerts scheduled. Everybody thought we would all be back home within a year. Instead a year later we were on our first mission trip to Faith Hope and Love Centers in Mexico City.

Then moving onto other nations our outreach grew into 30 + years of music and missions. We witnessed amazing miracles that would take a book to tell. So...From 1981 until 2014 we traveled in music and mission (evangelism) to 38 different nations, many of them religiously prohibitive or governmentally oppressed. We saw over 200,000 people come to Christ, gave away and smuggled over 400,000 Bibles in 11 different languages; majority in Chinese, Nepalese and Russian.

In 1982 we visited The Tabernacle in Orchard Park NY and met Pastor Tommy Reid. By 1984 it became my home church and still is today. It has always been my belonging place.

I am a small girl from a small town from a small minded family. How did this all come to pass? The difference is God's determination to save me, His Spirit empowering me, a new identity in Him and a destiny fulfilled that He decided way ahead of time. My promise is to follow God and His promise to use my life. It is a glorious collaboration; a covenant to lean, not on my own strength, but to trust Him and He will direct my path.

Lavon

"I will praise You, O Lord, among the peoples; I will sing to You among the nations." Psalm 57:9

REASON # 36

HE HEALS ME

Being a baby Christian, I didn't know anything about anything! But the church I went to at the time, Anchorage Christian Center, had miracles happening just about every week! One day my roommate, a recovering coke addict, came home with the flu. I said, "Hey man! The Bible says if you believe in the name of Jesus you can lay your hands on the sick and they will recover! You want me to pray for you man?" He said sure. So I laid my hand on his throat and prayed against the sickness in the name of Jesus. All the symptoms instantly disappeared!

We got so full of joy we started high-fiving each other, high-fiving Jesus, high-fiving angels!! We were just high-fiving everybody! The next evening he showed up at my church with his girlfriend who was on crutches. He said "Hey man – do that laying on the hands thing with Cory!"

She had been in an accident, and I saw the crutches so I prayed for her muscles, tendons, ligaments in her legs – but she walked out of the church still limping! I was a bit disappointed because I just KNEW God would heal her! But He knew what I didn't know!

That was a Wednesday night. Friday evening she showed up at the apartment, and I said "I want to pray for you again! I don't know why God didn't heal you!" Shane got all excited "Tell him! Tell him!! It turns out she was scheduled for surgery Thursday morning. She had a blood clot going up one of her arteries and it was getting very close to her heart which could have caused a heart attack. When she got to the hospital, they took the x-rays, and the blood clot was gone! So I prayed for her legs again that night – and they went out dancing! Totally healed!

Bill

*"O LORD my God, I cried out to You
and You healed me." Psalm 30:2*

REASON # 37

HE IS BY
MY SIDE

The day my mother told me she had been bleeding, I remember my whole world just stopped and I began to shake.

I was afraid I was about to lose my closest friend. My mom was just turning 70 and I wasn't ready to say goodbye to her. She was admitted to the hospital very weak, and the doctor told us to get her life in order as they expected the worse. They would be doing a long 6 hour surgery, and they didn't believe her chances of surviving were good.

On the way home, with my two sisters in the car, things were just about to get worse. Now the focus was on our survival, as we barely escaped a head-on collision. I must have looked away from the road, because before I knew it I was driving straight toward another car head on. I felt a strong inner strength that made me swerve away and get back into my own lane, just before our two cars hit. I believe God came to my rescue that day because I had a lot more life to live, and my family needed me!

That evening my son noticed how upset I was, and gave me a phone number for a religious television program, which staffed people who would pray for me. I gave that number to my sisters as well, and each of us called the number individually. Each person who prayed for us on the other line, told us the same thing…

"The doctors would be amazed!" Truthfully, I don't think we believed it because the doctors were so certain that her prognosis was not good. The surgery was scheduled immediately, and as we sat there in the waiting room we were prepared to be there for the long haul. But after about one hour of surgery, the doctors came out with their hands up in the air saying she is a healthy woman... and you can take her home tomorrow! The prayer counselors

were right, the doctors were all amazed! God didn't just save my mom's life that day... He had saved all of us that week! I can honestly say, that this was the first time in my life I had ever felt that close to Jesus. He revealed Himself to me as a friend, and His nearness was undeniable. He was at my side the whole time, taking care of my family, and watching over me.

Dorothy

"No longer do I call you servants, for a servant does not know what his master is doing; but I have called you friends."

John 15:15

REASON # 38

HE GUIDES MY
EVERY
DECISION

It is incredible to think that God cares about the small details of our lives, but He does. He will help us with every decision we need to make, if we just ask Him for His help. His Word assures us, "The Lord supplies ALL of our needs". Isn't that incredible! This next testimony is possible, because someone did just that... asked God for help when they needed to make a decision.

I remember the time we were driving an old, beat-up truck with no heat that someone had given us. We were thankful we had transportation, but having no heat meant we had to drape blankets over our laps in the winter to keep us warm. At the time, Herb was looking for work and that vehicle was essential part of getting him a job. I find it very interesting how God gives us just what we need, when we need it, and no sooner.

Well, Herb landed the job. But we quickly learned, that our truck was not proving to be the reliable transportation we needed. One morning, as Herb drove to work, he looked in the rear view mirror to see sparks flying! They were coming from our truck! As it turned out, there was a hole in the gas tank. Herb turned around and drove home and we started searching for a different vehicle that day.

That is how we found our little red car. The down payment was far beyond the $500 we'd somehow managed to save. But God intervened with a wonderful surprise! He led someone at our church to give us the down payment, we needed. We drove and drove that car all over Buffalo, even back and forth to Pittsburg, Pa. monthly. It was so comfortable and easy to drive. But, eventually, it wore down and needed to be replaced too. The body was rusted out and the engine was on its way out too, but I loved that little car.

By this time, we'd saved $1,000 as a down payment for our next car, and we started car hunting again! So many choices! It took us about 6 months to finally make a decision on the make and model. The first dealership turned us down, then the second and third. I even made Herb drive to Rochester because I saw a commercial on TV, from a car dealer who gives anyone a deal. Well, not us. I had to drive back and retrieve my $1,000 down payment when they finally admitted they couldn't help us.

Shortly after this, I was feeling dejected, and had a conversation with my Dad (Father God). It went something like this… "You know we really need a new car. Well, not brand new, but one that will get us to where we need to go. I know you have a reason for this delay God, and I have no problem staying in our little red car, but you have to keep it running because we can't afford to keep putting money into it. So if you keep it running for me, I'll stop looking and drive this one."
Silence…then God told me, "Drive to Towne right now." (Towne Ford, a dealership). And, of course I whined, "God I'm in Irving now and Towne is all the way in Orchard Park". Well, He simply said, "Go to Towne NOW". And I said "Fine!" So, I pulled into a parking lot and turned around, and started to drive back to

Orchard Park. When I got there I started browsing the car lot. I spied a Little Yellow Ford Escape, the exact truck I was looking for! So, I go in and tell the first staff member I saw... "I'm buying the Little Yellow Ford Escape out front." I didn't tell her I was interested in it, or that I'd like to test drive it, or even how much is it? I just simply said, "I am buying it." The salesman looked at me, peaked out the window at the truck, and proceeded to tell me, that they just received it an hour ago, so they hadn't even had time to check it over. He had no idea how much they wanted

for it. But, within 24 hours, I was driving my new Little Yellow Ford Escape off the lot!

The best part was that God gave me so many extras I didn't even know I wanted: CD player, step rails on both sides of vehicle and even a sunroof! Oh, did I mention it was the exact price God and I decided we could afford, to the very penny??? Well, He did it!

I've learned, when we let God lead, and obey His voice, His plans are so much better than our dreams. He takes such wonderful care of us and has always provided for us, although not always in the way we thought. Much of the time I just have to say, "Okay, God, I give up. I am not going to try and control this. I'm just giving it all to you and asking you to sort it all out." This gives Him the opportunity to create miracles in my life... and He continually does!

Herb and Alison

"Trust in the Lord with all your heart, and lean not on your own understanding." Proverbs 3:5

REASON # 39

HE KNOWS MY
NAME

One night, while sitting on a bar stool, with pool stick in hand, out of nowhere I began to ask myself, "My life revolves around this?" Then, two weeks later, while riding my 1968 Harley, that was strictly a Kickstarter - I like that, made me think I was a real biker! Heck, I didn't even have a tattoo… LOL! I made it part way through the intersection and was broadsided by a person going 30 to 40 miles an hour. Oddly enough, I got up from that accident, walked over to the bike, and rolled it over to the side of the road by the forks because the handlebars had come completely off. The handlebars had knocked out half the windows of the vehicle that hit me!

I sat down on a big boulder on the side of the road next to my bike. There was not a scratch on me. It was like the angels carried me in their arms and laid me safely on the ground. Later when I came back to the accident scene, the boulder was gone. How could this be? I'm not sure how to explain all that happened that day, but I do know it led me to think about my 2 ½ year old daughter that I hadn't been permitted to see for 6 months.

I called my former wife to tell her that I had almost died, and wanted to see my daughter, but all she said was that bad things happen to bad people, and good things happen to good people.

At the time I believed her, so I went to church that following Sunday. It was a church I had heard of that welcomes bikers so I thought I would give it a try. When I got there I noticed that I was the only one that had long hair and in leather. I realized I had gone to the wrong church, but it was no accident that I ended up there.

They had a play going on called "Heaven's Gate – Hell's fire." It was Easter and I didn't even realize it. After the play they said, if you want a different life come forward. That was the exact reason I was there. Not to get straightened out but to have a different life. It felt like somebody pushed me up from the back row... the Holy Spirit now had my full attention! As I knelt down I heard the minister pray in a strange language over the guy next to me. What the heck is that I thought? When he got up to leave so did I, and the minister said, "Brother I haven't prayed for you yet." I said, "That's okay, I felt that, and that's cool." I wasn't joking because I really did feel it... It felt like electricity coming through to me as he was praying for the man next to me! Then the man said, "Brother, can I pray for you?" So he prayed for me in that same strange language. After that, I remember getting up and feeling much lighter.

I was happier, and everything was brighter. And the rest is history! I now attend church weekly, and have found that good things can happen to anyone, because God truly is good and He does care!!

John Swiniarski

"The Lord is not slack concerning His promise, as some count slackness, but is longsuffering toward us, not willing that any should perish but that all should come to repentance."
2 Peter 3:9

REASON # 40

HE HEARS MY PRAYERS

I was on the way to an event with my mother in my hometown in New York. As we drove, I saw a man in distress lying on the sidewalk outside of the Catholic Church, where just moments before he had been worshipping. My mom spun the car around and I jumped out. Six people were taking turns administering CPR to this motionless man whose pulse had stopped for several minutes.

I found out his name was Jim. At one point his eyes opened and I kept looking into his blue eyes and touching his forehead. I was praying in tongues out loud, as the others stood by. I kept saying, "Jim, you will LIVE and NOT die!" After several minutes went by, Jim's eyes blinked and he sat up! The six other people from the church, that were around Jim indicated they were nurses, and they were all amazed how quick Jim came back to life and sat up as if nothing happened. Just minutes earlier his pulse had stopped and he was motionless! Glory to God our healer!!

Glory

… And by His stripes we are healed… Isaiah 53:5

REASON # 41

HE TEACHES ME
TO LOVE

I was only five years old when God first began to move in my life. At this young age I needed to hear that God loved me. I can honestly say, it was a time in my life that made me who I am today! God knew how much I would need Him early on in life, and He wanted me to know just how much I was loved. I lived in North Tonawanda in the projects across the street from Spruce Park. One day during the summer, an unexpected surprise occurred. The Salvation Army was putting on a wonderful party for the children in the neighborhood. It was here that I heard a message that would change my life forever. It was explained to me that I have a Heavenly Father who is always there for me, right inside my heart. He would be with me for every single thing I went through in life... and all I had to do was talk to Him. They told me that there would be troubles in my life but that they were all a part of my destiny. One day, after school, when I was just in kindergarten, I came home to find my front door was locked. There was a sign on the door, but I could not read, so I just kept trying to get in, but a neighbor saw me and told me that my mom, who was pregnant, was in the hospital. My dad and I went to the hospital, and the other kids stayed with a neighbor. We were told by the doctor and the Chaplin that my mom and my brother were both going to die because of all the complications with the birth. I remembered right away, that my Heavenly Father

123

did miracles. I thoroughly, totally, and completely believed that He would save my mom and my baby brother and all I had to do was pray and believe. Within 24 hours my mom and my brother we're doing just fine and both lived free from complications of any kind. God really does care! There were more times in my life when I had to trust God to watch over me and my family, but I will have to save those stories for another time. Truthfully, my life wasn't easy, but God was always by my side. His peace kept me calm when my dad, who had Schizophrenia, became violent. God's courage kept me strong when social services split my family up and put us in foster care. My sister and I were placed in the hands of cruel caretakers, but it was by God's grace and mercy that my family was reunited after years of separation. I was once again home with my mom and dad.

I think it is very important to say that I prayed every single day, and never gave up hope no matter what happened. I have to say that I am so thankful to God for the Amazing Power of Love that He gave to me, and the extraordinary power of forgiveness... never once did I ever have a problem thinking about what had happened in my past. To God be the Glory!

Terri DiNatale

"And we know that all things work together for good to those who love God, to those who are the called according to His purpose."
Romans 8:28

REASON # 42

HE DOES THE
IMPOSSIBLE

Back in Buffalo I was going to a church and met a guy, Jon, and he and I became friends. When I first met him he was in a shoulder cast from an accident, and we started praying together. A few weeks later when he got the cast off, the doctor told him he would never be able to lift his arms above his shoulders. Jon said "Like this!" And he shot his arms straight up over his head! The doctor looked at him and said "YOU CAN'T DO THAT!" He said, "I can't do what, this?" And he shot his arms straight up again! The doctor said "You don't understand!!! The mechanics of your body!!! How can you do that?" Jon answered him… "Me and my buddy have been praying and Jesus healed me!"

Another time, Jon called, and was in a panic state, he just said, "They found an aneurysm on my brain, they say it's serious, they're rushing me to a specialist now – I need you there praying!" So I said all right and he gave me the address. All the way there I was praying in the Spirit. When I got to the office he was already in the back room with the doctor – it was serious!

So I sat in the waiting room, flipping through some magazines, praying in the Spirit. I was there for about 45 minutes when I went up to the window and asked if they knew how long he would be. The girl said "He's going to be there a while! He's got three other doctors back there with him right now!" I thought to myself, I've got to get going, so I walked out saying "Thank You Jesus for healing him!"

It turns out, the reason he had three other doctors back there with him, when they took the MRI at this clinic – was because they couldn't find the aneurysm! The other doctors were looking things over, maybe they could see something that he wasn't! Could it have moved? The answer… it was totally gone! So they sent him home! Jesus is our healer!

Bill

"It is good to give thanks to the Lord, and to sing praises to Your name, O Most High; To declare Your loving kindness in the morning, and Your faithfulness every night." Psalm 92:1,2

REASON # 43

HE NUMBERS
OUR DAYS

I was on my way to pick up and deliver some work for the company which I was employed. Just ahead of me I saw a tire rolling down the Highway in my lane. As I was thinking someone lost their tire, little did I know that someone was me!

My vehicle began to fishtail back and forth across both lanes of the highway. I looked in my rear view mirror and there was an eighteen wheeler that pulled out of his lane onto the center of both lanes to keep the other traffic from passing until my vehicle was safely on the shoulder of the road out of danger. God sent an Angel in an eighteen wheeler to save my life. I am sure that I would not have survived to share this testimony if not for God's Divine intervention.

A. Smith

"For He shall give His angels charge over you, to keep you in all your ways." Psalm 91:11

REASON # 44

HE BLESSES ME

My first experience breeding dogs was quite spiritual. A friend of mine, Kathy, breeds Cavalier King Charles Spaniels. I always had an interest in dog breeding and this breed is awesome! I asked Kathy to join me in breeding a litter. Before I even got my first female Tricolor, I had a vision that I was going to have a male Tricolor and name him Brighton. When I saw this vision I thought, "Well, maybe down the road, but not for a while." I purchased my first female Cavalier King Charles Spaniel from Kathy and named her Bristol. When she reached maturity, I told Kathy I hoped to breed her with a male she had that was not of the same bloodline. While I waited for Bristol to reach maturity, I wondered why Kathy didn't have me come and help her whelp a litter. She gave me a book about breeding but it wasn't very extensive on the subject. So I arranged for Sue, another friend who lived closer, to help me. Sue had many years of breeding experience, in addition to show experience with Westies and Scotties, and assured me she would assist me.

Bristol went into labor on Sunday evening and labored all night. Kathy did not offer much help over the phone and she lived 2 hours away. I called Sue, only to find she had the flu and would not be able to assist me, after all. I stayed awake with Bristol all night and took her to the Vet the next morning. The contractions had stopped and the Vet said they were only Braxton Hicks (pre-labor contractions). I did not believe that, since she was just one day shy of her due date. The Vet assured me it would still be a couple of days. Later that day, I was talking to my mother on the phone, when all of a sudden Bristol's tail went up. It went up again and this time a puppy emerged! She had them very quickly, one right after the other, which is not usual. I had to catch them with a mitt! A total of six puppies in all!!!

All of the puppies were quickly spoken for save one, my favorite. As the weeks passed, although adorable, the puppies really had me hopping. So, as their nine-week adoption-ready milestone drew near, I was ready for them to go to their new homes. At nine weeks, Kathy came to pick them up to take them back to her house, as she arranged for most of them to be sold. The Tri-color (my favorite), Charles as I called him, was left with me. We tried to find him a home and thought we had, but the girl wasn't able to take him, after all. Another family came, but really wanted a Blenheim, as they had previously. A retired couple told Kathy they were interested in Charles. They drove to my house to meet him. By this time Chares was three months old and, unbeknownst to me, we had already bonded. (As I expressed earlier, Charles had always been my favorite.) But I did not realize how attached I had actually become to him until he was gone. The couple was very nice. They liked Charles and decided to take him but, as they put him in the car, I was crying. After he was gone, I would walk into each room and cry, remembering how he played in there…ate in there… slept with me and the other dogs in there…for what seemed like a lifetime.

My coworkers knew I wanted him back and finally encouraged me to contact the owner, to ask if she would consider giving him back. I knew she would say no and she did. The couple loved him and he was a good puppy. I continued to be depressed. To add to my sadness, I was dealing with a nasty co-worker and much spiritual warfare with that situation. It was all coming down on me and my attention turned to my job situation. After a month or so, I finally gave up on ever getting Charles back.

Until one morning, about six weeks later, when the lady who'd adopted Charles called. She asked if I still wanted him back. I asked her what was wrong with him. She said nothing but she was allergic to him! She was living on Benadryl and her quality of life was terrible. They'd always had a Shi Tzu, so she didn't know she was allergic to dogs. I was in complete shock! She brought Charles back. And, although my heart felt for her in having to give him up, I felt so blessed and happy to have him again! I realized, when I let Charles go, God gave him back to me...a lesson in putting something else first before Him. I gave up control and handed the situation over to God. Then, He blessed me with the sweetest puppy who is still bringing me joy and laughter. He was and is *my Brighton, the very same handsome Tri-color male I'd seen in the vision!*

Julie Tedesco

"Blessed shall you be when you come in, and blessed shall you be when you go out." Deuteronomy 28:6

REASON # 45

HE TOUCHED
ME

Following college graduation, I moved to the Mid-West to begin my teaching career. While I enjoyed the bustling growth of the oil boom in the city of Tulsa, Oklahoma, I developed terrible year-round allergies. Nothing relieved the symptoms and the only medications available at the time caused severe drowsiness. The groggy symptoms I experienced with them caused me to avoid taking them as often as needed.

When my parents came to visit, I took them to my church in southern Tulsa, Grace Fellowship, pastored by Bob Yandian. Suffering badly that day from allergies, I felt miserable. I told my parents I really hoped they would have an altar call at the end of the service for healing. As the service closed, Pastor Bob called all in need of physical healing to the front. I went, and he and his wife Loretta each placed a hand on either side of my head, as they prayed with me. While I sensed the presence of God throughout the service, and at the altar, I wasn't quite sure if I experienced the manifestation (proof) of my healing at that exact moment.

As the days passed I forgot about my allergies, and it hit me that they were gone! I had not experienced any symptoms since the Sunday service when Pastor Bob and Loretta laid hands on me! I am so grateful for the grace of God to heal me. I have remained free from allergies ever since!

Leslie

Heal me, O Lord, and I shall be healed; Save me, and I shall be saved, for You are my praise. Jeremiah 17:14

REASON # 46

HE HEARS ME

The Bible tells us, "God is our refuge and strength, an ever present help in trouble." (Psalm 46:1) This verse speaks about the omnipresence of God; that His power is able to transcend time and place, and meet us wherever we are. He can show up in a church pew...hospital bed...or, surprisingly, outside ...in the middle of the street.

After many years of heavy lifting at work, I found myself unable to bend down or walk far without severe pain in my back and running down my leg. My normal daily activities came to a halt and I had to leave work. I saw a Neurosurgeon who highly recommended surgery. He told me, that if I didn't have surgery, within five years, I would probably be confined to a wheel chair. Never walking again was not an option for me. I prayed to God and knew in my heart, no matter what the outcome, He would take care of me. So, I opted to have the surgery.

A week later, going for surgery, I was optimistic, confident God would be with me and guide the surgeon's hands. Surgery went well but I awoke to severe pain. And due to excruciating pain from the staples in my back Morphine became my daily companion. I was buzzing the nurses every hour to roll me over. That's when a Physical Therapist was assigned to teach me how to roll over; I'm sure this was a relief to the nurses. After 10 days in the hospital, I was able to walk. I was discharged and sent home for six more weeks of bed rest to continue the healing process. While recovering, my goal was to read the Bible from cover-to-cover; and so I began my journey. It took me longer than I thought, but I did it!

While recuperating, I realized I had three numb toes on one foot. So I cried out to God to heal me completely. He replied, "Get up and make your bed." I didn't understand what He was doing, but I did as He asked. Days later, full feeling came back to my toes. God wanted to be sure I would obey Him, even in the little things.

Several weeks later, I saw the doctor again. I walked into his office with both legs numb, from knees to ankles. My heart sank as the he told me this may be permanent. During surgery, he had to remove vertebrae, so some nerves may have been severed. As I left the office, I was devastated! My Spirit cried out, "I can't live like this!" The numbness was horrible. As I walked home from the doctor's office, it traveled up my legs to my thighs. Now, both legs were completely numb! I cried out to God right there... *in the middle of the street telling Him I couldn't live this way and to take this from me.* As I cried out, I felt the numbness leave my body! Praise God! He met me right where I was and *healed me* before I even got home – 100%. His love knows no bounds! The Lord is my healer!

Gail B.

"I cried out to the Lord because of my affliction, and He answered me" Jonah 2:2

REASON # 47

HE PROVIDES

At four years old, I watched a "Feed the Children" fundraiser, on television. The little girl in the video was covered in dirt. The only clean part of her was where the tears trickled down her little cheeks. I still remember how frail her arms and legs looked. Yet, in my innocence, her distended belly looked like she had more than enough to eat. It was then, that my mother had to explain to me what it meant to be malnourished. That moment so touched my young, tender heart that I proceeded to unwrap a piece of cheese and stuff it in an envelope. I knew mail came and went in envelopes somehow. I placed the cheese-filled envelope into my top drawer, then forgot about it. As you can imagine, my mother was not thrilled when she found it about a month later. This was the first call on my life to feed the hungry.

Fast forward to adulthood... About three years ago, two days prior to the annual Eagles Wings East Coast Leadership Conference, I sent a donation to Abraham's Bread, founded by Eagles Wings Ministry. Abraham's Bread helps feed the poor in Israel who have been affected by the devastating effects of poverty. I sent my donation in on a Monday, and the conference began on Wednesday. By Thursday, I was told, after months of waiting for a consignment item to sell, that it finally sold for $150! I ended up sowing most of that back into Eagles Wings during the conference. As timing would have it, I found out that my daughter's truck broke down, requiring $1600 in repairs. As a divorced single parent, I panicked! My only thought was, "Now, we'll have to use her college savings." After all, she couldn't be without transportation. Friday morning at 7:39 am, while driving to work and praying, I told God that He needed to make the impossible, possible. I left it in His hands and continued to work. By 11:30 am, my Grandmother called, to inform me she was buying my daughter a vehicle! And not just any vehicle...brand new! By Monday, that vehicle was sitting in our driveway, completely paid for!

It's no coincidence that when we choose to give, God opens the windows of heaven for us! His word says that in proportion to what we give it will be measured back to us. But God's measure comes back pressed down, shaken together, and running over! God is our Jehovah Jireh... our provider!

Faith and obedience are key elements to serving God. After all, without works, faith is dead. My children and I continue to pray for and support Eagles Wings and harvest much fruit as we bless God's Chosen People, through this reputable and trustworthy ministry.

Kristin E.

"He who has pity on the poor lends to the Lord, and He will pay back what he has given." Proverbs 19:17

REASON # 48

HE IS WITH ME

Jesus has done so much in my life! Before coming to the Lord, for three years, I was addicted to every prescription painkiller you can think of. During that time, about 15 years ago, while working one afternoon I felt sick and began vomiting puddles of blood. I looked to Heaven and pleaded, "Please, don't take me now. I'm not ready!" I didn't know Jesus at the time, but I could sense someone was there with me, because I could feel His presence. After, the vomiting stopped, I regained my composure and continued on with my workday.

That night, I shared my experience with my girlfriend. She suggested going to the hospital, but being the stubborn man that I was, I refused. Next, she asked if I would attend church with her... I said yes. Upon entering the church, I instantly felt Jesus's presence! That day, I repented of my addiction, and prayed the "Sinner's Prayer." The emptiness was gone. That day, I walked out of church a free man! I have never felt the need to take another prescription drug again!! He filled the empty hole in my heart with his love and truth. Thank You, Jesus, for saving my life!!! Amen

Dear Friend, just as Jesus freed this writer from addiction, He can free you, too, by replacing the emptiness with love and truth. Jesus is truly all we need! It's a high you'll never want to come down from!

Joe Pike

Yea, though I walk through the valley of the shadow of death,
I will fear no evil; For You are with me;
Your rod and Your staff, they comfort me. Psalm 23:4

REASON # 49

HE SAVES

One of the greatest joys as a Christian happens when we get the opportunity to share our faith with someone. Anyone! It's because we know what happened to us when we met Jesus! It's as if the re-start button gets pushed and all things become new! This next testimony is all about sharing the miracle of Salvation…

One of the many blessings I received was to be able to witness for Christ at my younger sister's funeral. She had a very short term illness called Multiple Myeloma that took her life at the young age of 58. My other sister and I always knew she worshipped differently from us, and we wondered whether she had truly accepted Jesus as her Savior. We had decided to approach her one morning in the hospital, and as we walked into the room she stopped us dead in our tracks and with a pointing finger, as if she knew what we were about to ask, she said "I am okay with Him (meaning the Lord) and so are my husband and son." We knew she would be ok, and had made her peace with God.

At her funeral, it was obvious she had made a big impact on the lives of her coworkers and friends. So much so that we accepted condolences for the 3 hours that would lead up to her funeral. When it came time to share what was on our hearts, with the more than 200+ attendees that remained for her memorial service, I told them how we had walked with the Lord for more than 30 years and that we had to know before our sister left this world, if she knew Jesus. The Pastor nodded and said he had to ask her too. The Bible tells us there is only one mediator between God and man and that His name is Jesus. This message of hope, and an eternal existence with our Savior, is what we so deeply wanted to convey that day.

We will never know how our witness impacted the lives of the people that came to say goodbye to our sister that day, but one day in Heaven we will.

God loves us so much that He gives us Joy even in the midst of sorrow. I am so blessed to experience His great Joy.

Lori C. Avedisian

"Therefore, if anyone is in Christ, he is a new creation; old things have passed away; behold, all things have become new."

2 Corinthians 5:17

REASON # 50

HE CALMS MY FEARS

My daughter and I were given an opportunity to tour Europe with Girl Scouts. We just needed to raise the money. So we sat together with our troop and made plans to begin. We were excited to think we would be able to go to England, France, Italy and Switzerland. Yet there was something deep down inside of me that kept nagging at my heart that we shouldn't go. I wanted to back out, telling myself that we could be killed by a random shooter, or some violent attack. The months leading up to our trip I kept reading in the paper about people who were murdered by terrorists, just random attacks. I kept having these scary thoughts about losing my daughter, and losing my own life too.

It became like collecting pennies, you know the way you might find one on the street or sidewalk, or the pocket of an old coat. Well these thoughts became like the pennies, finding one after the other. Pretty soon my collection of negative thoughts began to spill over and were affecting the way I was feeling about the trip. The excitement of planning and my happiness about the tour was rapidly dwindling away. Finally, I sat down and prayed over my anxiety. I heard God's voice asking me to imagine myself going into a city on the tour, like London. Then, He asked me to describe how I was feeling seeing the people, being near some of the sights, like Big Ben, Windsor Castle, walking about, hearing the many different dialects of speech, smelling everything from foods to underground trains. I said I would feel: happy, interested, curious, intrigued, excited and amazed. That's when I knew I would enjoy myself, because I didn't answer in terror and sadness. I realized I had been listening to the wrong voice all along. The one that would have me miss out on the life that God had planned for me... abundant life! God's voice is one of happiness, encouragement, and trust. It leads me to a fulfillment of my greatest dreams. My pockets were full of doubts and fears. But God turned my pockets inside out and everything changed for me. I heard His calm voice.

Ann Crinzi

O God, You *are* my God; Early will I seek You; My soul thirsts for You; My flesh longs for You in a dry and thirsty land where there is no water. So I have looked for You in the sanctuary, to see Your power and Your glory. Psalm 63:1, 2

I'd like you to meet someone....

My name is Brendan McKirchy, and I am an Elder at Love Joy Church in Lancaster, New York and I am one of the leaders for Western New York Treasure Hunters. My parents are Rich and Virginia McKirchy who have led various ministries in Buffalo, New York. For the last six years Diane Miles (The Tabernacle), Damar Dowell (Vanguard), Jason Davis (Vanguard), and myself have led countless treasure hunts across Western New York. Each of us are normal everyday believers who have made a decision to take risks for Jesus Christ and see what He would do with our lives. No one should idolize us or think we have something that they don't have, because the truth is all of us have the same spirit that rose Christ from the grave (Romans 8:11).

Throughout my life, my parents and church, Love Joy, have inspired me to believe God for more. I remember when I was 11 years old my dad wanted to tell me about something that happened to him. Earlier that week he was praying in my living room when God showed him a street name and address in the city. He saw that it was a bar and then God showed him a calendar with the date circled, and a time on a clock. He then walked into the bar in this vision and met a man and talked to him for roughly an hour. A week later in real life, my dad showed up at that bar on that date and time, and saw the man. He walked over to him and said to him, "you don't know me, but God told me about you." He told the man everything God said. The man said, "Why did God tell you this?" My dad then said, "Because this is the only way you would believe God sent me here to tell you to save your marriage." The man started crying and said he came to the bar to get drunk and then he was going to go home and sign the divorce papers. As a kid, I saw things like this all the time. God consistently used both of my parents because they made their lives available to him. I said as a kid I want to hear You God, like they hear You so I too can be led by You in life. Ever since this prayer as a kid I have witnessed countless miracles because Jesus is as real and available to anyone who makes their lives available to Him.

Before treasure hunting I always had a heart to reach the lost. For years I would meet up with a group of 20-30 young adults and have very intimate encounters with God as we would do heart and bowl prayer and worship nights. I would leave there so full of God and ready to release the kingdom. The sad thing was that almost everyone else there wanted to live a OO7 Christian lifestyle. They wanted to go crazy about God behind closed doors, but be completely silent around the world. One night after a worship night everyone wanted to go to Dave and Busters at the mall. I asked if anyone wanted to pray for people in the mall and thankfully I had one friend, Josh Krampen, who was crazy enough to join me on an adventure into the unknown. We bound up any principalities or powers in the mall and sent them to the gates of hell until their day of judgment and we loosed heaven in the mall and asked for the Holy Spirit to highlight people. I had never done anything like this before, but I was excited to see what God would do. After walking around for above five minutes I noticed a lady on a bench and I felt the Holy Spirit highlight her. I started talking to her and found out that she was sitting on the bench while her whole family was there Christmas shopping at the Eastern Hills Mall because she had terrible back and knee pain. I told her if she let us pray for her the Bible says as we lay hands on the sick they will recover (Mark 16:17-18). I put my hand on her knee and Josh put his hand on her back. As I was praying I felt her knee popping. I then asked her to test it out. She started walking around and said "Jesus just healed my knee". Then she screamed out that Jesus had just healed her knee while crying. At this point a crowd was watching. I didn't know what to do because I had never been in this situation before. I asked her how her back was feeling. She said she still felt pain. I told her the Bible says as we keep asking, keep seeking and keep knocking the door will be open (Luke 11:9-13) and you will be healed. We prayed a second time over her back and asked her to test it out. She starts crying and screaming again saying her back is healed. People were still watching, but at the time we had no idea what to do next. We talked to the lady about Christ and thankfully she's a Bible believing Christian and we will see her again in Heaven. About a month later God connected me to Damar and Diane so we could all start taking risks together.

My lack of fruit motivated me to put myself in uncomfortable situations where God wanted me to go. I didn't hear God calling me to go to the mall to pray for people. I just knew his word said to go into all the world and preach the good news. Most of us use "I'm waiting for God to reveal His calling on our lives" as a means of avoiding action. My response to that mentality is this, did you hear God calling you to sit in front of the TV yesterday, or to go on your last vacation, or to exercise this morning? Probably not, but you still did it. The point is that Vacations, and exercise are not wrong, but that we are quick to rationalize our entertainment and priorities and we are slow to commit to serving Jesus Christ.

My challenge to all the believers that read these testimonies is that if you are willing to take a risk with Jesus you will see increase after increase of faith and movement of the Holy Spirit in your lives. I think it starts with being intentional with your calendar. Many people don't intentionally set aside time in their calendar to be used by God. I remember once someone told me that is legalistic and you should always be available to God. I agree that we should always be available, but I'm talking about 100% full focus missionary style commitment. This isn't easily accomplished unless you commit time in your calendar on purpose to serve the Lord. I personally am a very busy person and if I don't make time on my calendar where I say, "God do what you want to do every second of the four hours I am setting aside on this date and time" I won't do it. Most people reading this could reflect on the past ten years of their life and realize they never took any major risks for Jesus, prayed for people in public or tried to share the gospel with anyone. The most common thing you hear a believer say on their death bed is that they wish they spent more time with Jesus (Billy Graham recently said this on his death bed), and that they allowed Jesus to use them more in their lives. They never say, I wish I watched more TV, I wish I memorized more facts about sports, etc. All of these things are harmless, but they can lead you down a path where you miss your purpose. I remember hearing a testimony from one of the most famous witches in Africa that got saved years ago. Satan was showing these witches different forms of technology he was creating. What he described in his testimony was that Satan told him these pieces of technology were being created so believers would waste their lives messing around with the technology and not focusing on Gods purpose for their lives. When I read this testimony years ago it really impacted me to try to always remember that there are many things we can focus on in our lives that are totally harmless (ex Facebook, sports, videogames etc), but if they are keeping you from fulfilling the call of God on your life, through wasting your limited time on Earth it can be a bad thing.

This young man has inspired me… He has grasped the calling of the church… He has challenged us to believe we were created for greater things! I pray that these next 10 testimonies, devoted to "TREASURE HUNTING," will inspire you to ask God to use you in even greater ways too!

Jesus said to His disciples, "The harvest is great, but the workers are few. So pray to the Lord who is in charge of the harvest; ask Him to send more workers into His fields."
Matthew 9:37,38

Supernatural Evangelism

WHAT IS TREASURE HUNTING?

Treasure Hunting is Evangelism that uses a map to search for people, who are treasures to God. We just ask the Holy Spirit to guide us… We couldn't find these people without Him!

Here's what we do… a group of believers come together and worship Jesus for 30-45 minutes. But, before we do that, we ask Jesus to show us where He wants us to go that night. He gives us words of knowledge about locations and other unusual things. We write these down on a paper called our Treasure Map and go to the locations on this Map to find "treasures." The "treasures" are people who correspond in some way to the clues that the team has written down. We break up into groups of people (three to five per team) and combine the overlapping clues God laid on our hearts when we were praying and worshiping (ex: location, people's names, appearance and prayer needs). When we find someone, at the location God directs us to go, we explain and show them this map and ask if we can pray for them. Many people have been saved, healed, or delivered from demons, and greatly touched by God's love through this kind of evangelism. People many times are just overwhelmed at how clearly it was that God sent us to them. *Acts 9:10-19 is a great example of a biblical treasure hunt and how the Apostle Paul got saved!*

Brendan McKirchy & Jason Davis

Miracles 51-60

"CHINESE STUDENT LOOKING FOR JESUS"

The location God gave us was UB North Campus 'Center for the Arts', and Pool/water. The name He gave us was Peter. The unusual clue was red door.

This is what happened… So the group walked into the center for the arts having no idea how this would come together (especially the pool/water clue in the center for the arts). We soon discovered that the doors had different colors and one set of doors were red. So we walked through the red doors, and to our surprise there was an underground passageway to the gym (pool) in this building (none of us had any idea existed). So we decided to start walking down this long passageway. Along the way one person was approaching us. Our team introduced ourselves and his name was PETER. We then went on to offer prayer for him, but he didn't understand what prayer was.

He grew up in China and has been in the US for a year. Our team then explained we pray to Jesus. When we said the name "Jesus" he went crazy. He told us that his parents sent him to America to get an education, but also to find out who Jesus is. In the area he grew up in China it is dangerous to talk about Jesus. His first year at UB he would walk up to people and would ask them if they know about Jesus at UB, and so far all he has found out is that he was "a good man". Our team then walked him through the gospel and who Jesus was. He then said he wanted to accept Christ as his Savior. After accepting Jesus into his heart, he got plugged into a Christian group at UB that helps Chinese students learn English through studying the bible. Yes, all of us were stunned and blown away on how God directed the team that night. Peter was looking for truth, and God was looking for vessels to tell him about the truth. When the body of Christ steps out, God will make the connections!

"And how will anyone go and tell them without being sent? That is why the scriptures say, "How beautiful are the feet of messengers who bring good news!" Romans 10:15

THE MYSTIC SHOP

On this evening Diane Miles and four very tired friends came together for a Treasure Hunt. Little did they know that this was an evening that would change the course of their lives, and the lives of the treasures they were about to meet. After receiving clues and some words of knowledge from God, we headed out down Delaware Ave. until we found the spot the Lord was directing us to. A mystic shop run by a beautiful woman practicing palm reading, spiritual cleansing, and tarot cards. After entering the shop and introducing ourselves, we introduced her to the Truth and the Power of the One Holy Spirit. We led her through prayers of healing, salvation, forgiveness and deliverance.

She then called her husband on the phone who was out of town on business because he needed healing in his body. Over the phone we commanded healing into those sick areas. He was instantly healed....all pain gone. He then invited Jesus to be his Lord and Savior. While this was all taking place, two women were in the back of the store observing this encounter we had with God. We asked them if they would like to have some of what we were giving away, and they quickly came to join us in a circle. We released the Presence of God and they were healed. One accepted

Jesus as her Lord, and was set free from hurts of the past through prayers of forgiveness. Joy was released and one woman laughed again for the first time in many years. Jesus promised that if we declared the Kingdom of God is at hand.....He would extend His hand to heal with signs wonders and miracles.

Who would have known that in a mystic shop on Delaware Ave that night, there would have been three women and a man looking for the Truth...God knew. And The Truth walked into their lives and set them free!

One week after the mystic shop owner had this encounter, she closed the mystic shop and chose to pursue Jesus for the rest of her life. The Lord is our rescuer!

"Jesus looked at them and said to them, with men this is impossible, but with God all things are possible." Matthew 19:26

UNIVERSITY OF BUFFALO FOR JESUS

The team prayed and asked Jesus to guide us to the people he wanted us to minister to and these were the words of knowledge that God gave us for this night. The location God told us to go to was "weights" and "stop sign". What they needed prayer for was "deliverance from drugs". The unusual clues were "street, "circles", and "bus windshield". This is what happened...

Our team had went a few places around campus and released the love of Christ on a few people and shared Christ with some people that had literally never heard of Jesus or Christianity at UB (that's like the fifth time that has happened....it's a mission field). One of the last stops we felt led to go to was to the gym because of the "weights" word of knowledge. Since it was raining outside we were going through the tunnels to get from building to building, but the tunnel finally ended so we had to run outside in the rain. We went outside and as we were jogging to the gym (weights) a bus stopped at the "stop sign" in a "bus circle" in front of us. One of the members of the team thought "this is it", so we went into the bus. It was empty minus the driver. We asked the driver if we could pray for her and she seemed a little hesitant, and then I asked what was going on with her left leg because it was all wrapped up. She told us that she's in all kinds of pain in that leg and the doctors haven't been able to figure out exactly what's

154

wrong with her leg. She said she needed prayer for a lot of things and we said that we would be happy to pray for her about it if she felt like sharing it with us. Her heart had been heavy because she broke up with a co-worker, and couldn't open up to her friends because they were gossipers so she had closed herself off (she seemed down when we were talking). She was shocked that God would care to send us to her. We explained that He loved her outrageously and He's the good shepherd and a good shepherd runs to help a wounded sheep. We also explained that going through the mourning process is not a bad thing. The Lord had prepared me for this by just recently having me listen to a sermon on the necessity of temporary mourning in the healing process. Think of a little child. They get into a fight, cry and one minute later they are best friends with the person again. When you hold onto that stuff it causes you more pain than needed.

I then asked her if she had a friend or relative that had a drug addiction (it was one of our clues) because I believed it wasn't her, but someone she knew who had an addiction. She said her son had a drug addiction, and that morning she was actually praying for him to get free of it because she had been trying to be a better parent. The team prayed, that the King of Kings, and Lord of Lords would show up (Jesus!!!!), and her countenance was lifted. As the word says, "Blessed are those who mourn, for they will be comforted (Matthew 5:4)." She cried as we prayed and when it was over, the fruits of the spirit (Galatians 5:22-23) were on full display. Next, we asked her to try and do what she couldn't do before with her leg. She said the pain went from a 10 (being really bad) to a 3 (not bad) and then she took off the wrap and tested it further to find out that she was 100% healed!!!!! The women started testifying after about how amazing it was that her shift had just ended and she randomly decided to stop there to rest before

155

she brought the bus back to the drop off location. God is faithful to His word when He says that He will be a "lamp unto our feet" as He directly guided us to this wounded sheep.

"For thus says the Lord GOD: "Indeed I Myself will search for My sheep and seek them out. As a shepherd seeks out his flock on the day he is among his scattered sheep, so will I seek out My sheep and deliver them from all the places where they were scattered on a cloudy and dark day." Ezekiel 34:11,12

The location was Tops and aisle 7. The clothing: brown and red shirt. We heard Jesus say cane, hearing, peace, and restoration. The unusual clue was crackers. This is what happened...

So the group walked to Tops and went straight for Aisle 7. On the sign for aisle 7 it happens to say crackers as a major item in that aisle. We start to walk down the aisle and are blown away at what we saw. A women with a brown shirt and a cane was walking with her son who happened to have a red shirt on. The team approaches them and we break down why we are there, and we soon discover that the boy is deaf (the hearing clue). The woman explained that she needed a cane because she has Meniere's disease which causes extreme pressure in the persons head and causes them to be off balance and fall over when the pressure is very high. She then explained that she had just told her son that the pressure was so bad that they might need to leave Tops. Jesus changed that! The team prayed and the women's pain went from a 9 to a 3. We prayed a second time and it was almost completely gone. While we prayed a second time a spirit filled family happened to walk

157

down the same isle and joined us in praying for them.   The team then prayed for her sons healing, that he would have no more seizures and we have no doubt that our Good Father heard and honored our prayers!

"...The effective, fervent prayer of a righteous man avails much."
James 5:16

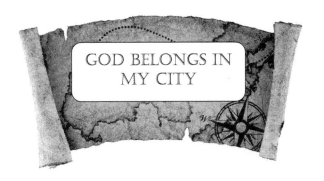

GOD BELONGS IN MY CITY

The location was Chippewa. The clothing was green shirt. The appearance was braids/dread locks. The issue that they needed prayer for was their job situation. This is what happened....

So the group walked down Chippewa and towards the end of the street, a man on a bike approached us wearing a green shirt and had braids/dread locks. Our team flagged him, and this other woman he was with down. They came over and I explained that we prayed that morning and the Lord showed us a man with dread locks/braids wearing a green shirt on Chippewa and that we were supposed to pray for them. The man then said, "Well, I'm looking for the love of my life, do you happen to be the love of my life?" (I'm a guy) I told him I loved him like a brother and he laughed with us (The girls noticed that his nails were painted. I'm a typical guy and didn't notice). I then explained, that earlier that day the Lord told me that I was going to pray for him about his job situation. The women and him were blown away because the night before they had talked about his job situation for a few hours because he's not sure if they are going to remove his position as a kindergarten teacher, and he has been doing that for 26 years. It was a huge source of stress in his life. The team prayed and as we did the Lord directed our prayer to a few other areas. After we finished the woman and the man explained that it was amazing that when we prayed we touched every area that they had talked about the night before. We explained that Christ did that because He wanted them to know that He cares about every detail of their life (1 Peter 5:7 "Give all your worries and cares to God, for he cares about you."). The man has been going to a catholic church down town, but this encounter really let him know that God is pursuing him and loves him!

"How precious are Your thoughts towards me, O God! How great is the sum of them!" Psalm 1309:17

JAW AT THE
WATERFRONT

The team prayed and asked Jesus to guide us to the people he wanted us to minister to and these were the "clues" that God gave us. The location God told us to go to was "The Waterfront". We heard Jesus say jaw/teeth. This is what happened...

While prepping to go treasure hunting, a treasure came into our church. Some of the members of "team 2" focused on him, and ministered to him, while "team 1" prepared to go out.

Initially "team 2" didn't have many clues (words of knowledge) as to what Jesus was going to lead us too, so we went to the waterfront and asked the Holy Spirit to highlight who he wanted us to minister too. Our team crossed over the Erie Canal Bridge and one member instantly felt led to approach someone on the other side of the bridge. He asked another group member if he felt led to approach anyone, and he said that guy over there. It was the same guy (there were probably 50 plus people in this area). So we approached him and said we were on a prayer walk and asked to pray for him. He said he was good and didn't need prayer. Then a member of the team said the Lord is telling me that you need pray for your jaw/teeth. The guy looks back in awe. He goes on to say that he has a bullet in his jaw by his teeth and the doctors can't get it out because it's by his jugular/corroded artery. He told us it has been a great source of pain, but he lives for pain. He then went on to say that praying for him might not make sense since he's Muslim. In that moment one of the team members got a word of knowledge that he used to go to church with his parents when he was a kid. Then went on to say that something happened to his parents and that resulted in him walking away (the root cause). The man then said that his dad was a Buffalo police officer and he got shot and killed. When it happened he said something inside of him died and he started to have a deep hatred for anyone who gave him trouble. At the same time he pretty much gave up on church. He said that if anyone messed with him he would mess them up.

He said when we approached him he was getting ready to pull a knife on us because we might be trouble. He said he served 25 years in jail for murdering someone who messed with him. He went on to say he has no direction in life and he didn't know what he is supposed to be doing. He said he has multiple sclerosis and Diabetes and his family always told him that he would get it because it's in their blood (generational curse). He said when his health gets worse he's just going to get drunk and blow his brains out. The team then told him that we would ask God to show us what he is supposed to be doing.

One team member gets a word for him that he has had trouble with relationships because he doesn't know how to love. He went on to tell him as he develops his relationship with God, who is love, he will learn to give the love that he has always wanted to give. The man agreed that what the team member said was 100% accurate. This team member went onto say that this guy tends to put on a tough front a lot, but he's actually very joyful. He tends to always be full of joy. God wants him to know that he made him that way and he wants him to show the joy that God has put inside of him. The guy laughs and again confirms that it's accurate.

Now it's prayer time. We lay our hands on him and the Holy Spirit starts to flow. One member is praying and God shows him a broken heart and that the Lord was mending it. Then the Lord laid an impression that this man has been spared through many situations where he should have died. Over and over people have told him it's a miracle that he is even alive. God kept him alive for this very moment (God's presence fell and the man started to chuckle confirming that what was said was right). We then spoke to the jaw. He told us that morning he forgot his meds so the pain was really bad. He then said the pain went from a 10 to a 3 (zero meaning no pain). We offered to pray again, but he said he didn't want to do it right then because this was blowing his mind.

He told us he had no direction on where to go with his life and we told him that we would ask God to show us what his next steps were supposed to be. God showed the team a vision of what God has called him to do. While praying for him one of the team members saw a picture of him dressed in a tie going to a corporate office downtown for work. He then went onto say he has studied law for 14 years and was considering pursuing the legal side of law enforcement. This encouraged him to start pursing that dream.

Just remember how this started. He said no to us. The power of a word of knowledge led to a conversation that lasted for well over an hour that most likely will have eternal implications for this man.

"Restore to me the joy of Your salvation, and uphold me be Your generous Spirit." Psalm 51:12

APPLE OF THE
FATHER'S EYE

The team prayed and asked Jesus to guide us to the people He wanted us to minister to, and these were the words of knowledge that God gave us. The location God told us to go to was "Macys" and "Apple". What they needed prayer for was "finances". This is what happened...

So the group walked through Macys on our way to the Apple store. Along the way to Apple the team ran into two friends, Amber N. and Andy C. They both said they would join us for a little while. The team walked into Apple and then one member saw a customer and felt like he needed prayer for his finances. Someone else in the group felt the same thing for that customer. So we approach him and said that we felt like Jesus wanted us to pray for his finances. He says it's accurate and he needs it. We try to talk more about Jesus, but he can't understand the words we are using because his first language is Spanish and he speaks limited English. The Lord then laid a prophetic word on one of the team members hearts for the man's girlfriend, but she didn't speak any English and had recently moved to the US from Puerto Rico. We asked God why he gave us this word for them if we have to end it here because of the communication gap. God responded... He said, I just gave you Amber N. and Andy C. Amber N. was a missionary in the Dominican Republic, and Andy C. was a missionary in Costa Rica, and both of them had learned Spanish.

We pull them into it. They start to translate the word in Spanish as it was given. "The Lord is showing me that when you were a little girl a powerful word was spoken over your life. Growing up everyone would look at you and say that's the girl (referring to the anointed call she has on her life). For years your Grandparents have interceded for breakthrough in your life, and you have seen God bring crazy breakthrough in some impossible situations, because of their intercession for your life." The women acknowledged that all of that was accurate. Then the Lord highlighted her son. "I see him holding a microphone and preaching the Gospel (his mom was holding back tears) and a lot of the warfare you have faced is because the enemy is afraid of the calling on this family's life." The team then told her that she might have walked off the path God was calling her, but God wants to direct her back onto His path for her.

The team said that God is like a GPS. The GPS system doesn't give you all the directions to go from New York City to San Diego all at once, because if it did it would be too much to comprehend. In this same manner God doesn't tell you everything he is going to do in your life because if he did, it would blow your mind. His plans are so huge for your life that if you received all of it at once you wouldn't believe Him. So God breaks it down for you and tells you the way to go one step at a time. You have to trust the

GPS one step at a time just like you have to trust God's direction for your life one step at a time. Along the way you might have made some wrong turns and the enemy keeps telling you that those wrong turns have resulted in you missing your calling, but the most amazing thing is His grace through the journey. God could tell you to go straight, but you choose to go right. When you finally turn around to go back the only thing you will hear is recalculating because he is rerouting you to your destiny. You may not deserve it, but that's God's grace. Then the team said "This is a divine moment and the Lord sent us here to remind you of the path you are called to walk down."

Then the boyfriend nudges the girl and said "Tell them the dream". The team said "Yes, tell us the dream!" This girl walked away from Christ years ago and she said "Last night I had a dream. In the dream I died. Then Jesus showed up. He reached down and brought me back to life. He then picked me up and said "I'm going to give you another chance to walk the road I have called you to walk into your destiny". Then we asked if they wanted to rededicate their lives to Christ. They all said "Yes!" They all are part of our family now and they are being plugged into a Spanish speaking church in Buffalo.

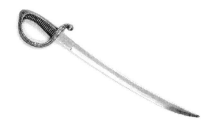

"For the gifts and the calling of God are irrevocable."

Romans 11:29

THE POWER OF HIS LOVE ON JULY 4TH

The team prayed and asked Jesus to guide us to the people He wanted us to minister to and these were the "clues" that God gave us. The location was Elmwood, Iron clad black gate, Tower, trees (2). The clothing: black shirt. We heard Jesus say forgiveness, relationships, and stomach pain. This is what happened...

The cool thing about this testimony is that this girl that took a risk to release this next word, had missed a golden opportunity a few weeks before on a treasure hunt, but learned from it. A few weeks ago on a treasure hunt, she sensed the Lord wanted her to tell this guy that God wanted to bring healing to his past. She heard God say that he had been kicked out of his house when he was 17, when he was 19 both of his parents died, and on top of that he lost his job. She held back, fearing she had misheard God.

The guy said he didn't want prayer for anything and walked away. As he was walking away someone in the group told the rest of the group that they know him. And when he was 17 he got kicked out of his house, when he was 19 both of his parents died and he just recently lost his job. I encouraged her and said now you know when the Lord is speaking to you, and I encourage you to take risks when you hear him! Here's what happened the next time she felt God speaking to her...

We already knew we were going to Elmwood, and we felt like we should start right around Buffalo State. When one of the members of my team got "iron clad black gate", "trees", and "tower" it was confirmation that we would be going to Elmwood and would start by the Buffalo Psychiatric Center. So we parked the car and started walking around the Buffalo Psychiatric Center looking for the person that God was sending us to. As we got to the end, one member of the team felt that we needed to keep going around. It looked like we were fenced in that way, but there happened to be one opening so we could get back to the street. Our team started walking down the street towards "Elmwood" as we walked there were a handful of people outside, all of sudden one of the members sees someone getting out of a car across the street that happened to be wearing a black shirt and felt a strong tug from the Holy Spirit to approach them. The conversation started out a little rough. We asked if we could pray for them in any way. The person said "Everyone can use prayer. Why don't you pray for peace in the world." I then broke it down to them why we specifically approached them and told them the testimony about the guy wearing the green shirt on Chippewa last week so he understood we don't just cast our nets at everything possible. We cast as Jesus leads since we asked Him to lead! So he opens up a little, and says he has some pain in his body. Obviously we asked where it was. He said it was in his stomach.

I then asked what was going on and he said he has had acid reflex ever since he got shot in the stomach. He then told us he also needed prayer for his heart because he got shot a few centimeters from his heart and has had some problems ever since. I then pressed again and asked if there was anything else and the girl and guy looked at each other and said "our relationship". I then told them (and showed them on paper) that the Lord told us that the person would need prayer for their relationship and part of it was related to forgiveness. They confirmed it was them. The man went on to tell various stories of people who have seriously wronged him, some of them sadly were from the church. Our group then explained to the man that we would be his worst enemy if we didn't tell him that he must forgive those that have wronged him. Our team walked him through the parable in Luke 23 and how if he will not forgive them then he will not be forgiven. The team also had various testimonies where they could relate to this couple (oddly in almost every situation). The Lord truly uses everything we go through for our good and His glory. The guy and girl looked at each other and agreed he needed to forgive them.

The girl had a solid foundation in Christ, but the guy seemed to only have a partial foundation. It was mainly due to terrible representatives of Jesus (wolves in sheep's clothing). Then it came time to pray. The team prayed and after our first prayer session, the man said his feet were on fire and it was as if the acid reflex problem had just went through his body out his feet (praise Jesus!). After a few of us prayed I asked the other girls in our group if they had anything the Lord had laid on their hearts for this couple. That's when this girl released a powerful word of knowledge to the girlfriend. The guy was very protective of her so she didn't really open up or do much talking, but Jesus wanted her to know he loved her. The girl on our team said "The Lord told me he wants you to know He sees what's going on between you and your mom (instant opening of floodgates and this girl starts balling, and the guy she's with is blown away). He wants you to know that HE HEARS YOUR EVERY PRAYER. The way your mom treats you is not the way God desires you to be treated. He loves you so much and "HEARS YOUR EVERY PRAYER." Then this girlfriend starts testifying how dead-on the word of knowledge was. The girl told us she has been praying about this borderline abusive situation and that morning she asked God "Do you even really hear me still?" (she used to have a close relationship with Christ, but has walked away a little bit). In her head she decided that He didn't hear her and it was time to give up on God. Then God sent the team to let her know He had heard her.

They start testifying to how crazy it was that we even ran into them. She was dropping off her boyfriend and was in a hurry to get out of there. If the team wouldn't have been obedient to the voice and walked around the Buffalo Psychiatric Center, we wouldn't have been in the exact right place at the right time right when she was dropping off her boyfriend. We would have missed this whole encounter. They want to maintain a relationship with us and it turns out the guy is part owner of the famous Niagara Café and he wants us to stop by and have some food and continue to talk about Jesus and testify to some other things he didn't want to go into detail about at that time, about the significance of what just happened (we were talking with them from 1:00 am to roughly 3:00 am).

But as it is written:

"Eye has not seen, nor ear heard,
Nor have entered into the heart of man
The things which God has prepared for those who love Him."

1 Corinthians 2:9

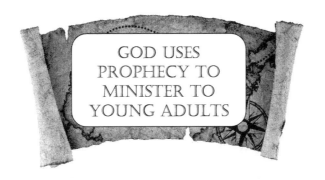

The team prayed and asked Jesus to guide us to the people He wanted us to minister to and these were the words of knowledge that God gave us for this testimony. The location God told us to go was "Galleria Mall" and "Microsoft store" along with a "bench". The appearance clues were "red shoes". This is what happened...

The group is headed to the Microsoft store in the Galleria Mall. As the group is on the way, two of them stop to talk a man in the mall that matches some of our other clues. As they are talking, the other group notices four young adults all wearing red shoes and they go into a store across the hall. When the other group finishes up talking with the man, everyone sees the group of young adults in red shoes leave the store and sit down on a bench in front of the Microsoft store. This is the treasure they were after.

The group approaches the young adults and tells them they are God's treasure and that God highlighted them that night to tell them how much He loves them. The leader of the group says "I am an atheist and I don't believe in God."

But just prior to encountering these young adults, two of the members in our group were sharing a story of how they heard a message of a preacher encountering a man who said he was an atheist, and here's how he responded... "My God is bigger than that." God then spoke to the preacher about the man in front of him, and God told him detailed things about him. This group tried the same thing. The group asked the man if they could ask God to tell them things about him and prove that He is real. The man obliged. They group started praying and God said, "You were really smart growing up but people began to speak negatively over you and tear you down and then your grades started to suffer." His eyes got wide as he responded "Yes! How did you know that?" Then another person in the group feels God say "Your parents are divorced and God wants to restore that relationship." The young man opens his mouth wide in disbelief. "Yes, that's true too. This is weird. How do you know this?" What the man receiving prayer didn't know is the second word was almost not given. The other member in the group felt God lay on their heart about God restoring the divorce in the house, but was afraid if he released the word and it was wrong that it would negate the whole thing. Thankfully, in faith and by God stirring in their heart, the word was released and gave this young man hope, and even more confirmation that God is real, and He does care.

One girl in the group then shouted "Pray over me next!" Excitement grew within the group and God gave everyone specific words to each one of the young adults that ministered to their hearts. They all enjoyed the time we spent with them. God clearly showed up to each one of them in powerful ways. While they didn't accept Jesus at that moment, God marked them with a moment in their lives they will never forget. The group planted the seed and God will bring the increase.

"Today I will hear His voice and harden not my heart"

Psalm 95:7,8

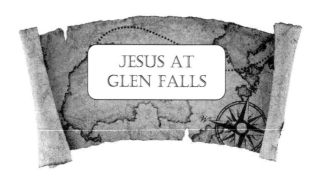

JESUS AT
GLEN FALLS

The team prayed and asked Jesus to guide us to the people He wanted us to minister to and these were the words of knowledge that God gave us for this testimony. The location God told us to go was "Glen Falls." The appearance clues were "20 year-old man", "Dark outfit" and "dark short hair". What they needed prayer for was "metal in body causing pain", "knee pain", "ankle pain" and "fear and anxiety." This is what happened....

The group arrived at Glen Falls. Upon entering the park, they notice a couple together and the man fits the description perfectly. He looks about 20 years old, is wearing a dark outfit and had short dark hair. When the group attempts to go over to the couple they turn a corner and are nowhere to be found. They decided to continue looking for other clues while they are there and believe God will bring the couple back to them.

At the end of the time at Glen Falls, they head back up the hill to the car and the couple comes walking down the hill. The group sends two people over to them and tells them how God highlighted them with the clues and loves them so much. The couple is open for prayer and tells the group that they both have knee and ankle pain and the girlfriend needs prayer for fear and anxiety. They look at our treasure map and see other prayer needs they have as well. The boyfriend also tells the group that he is twenty years old as well. Confirmation of all the clues we had.

First, the group starts praying for the boyfriend. He receives healing in his knee and ankle and is completely shocked about what is happening. Then he tells us that his back needs prayer as well because it's in a lot of pain. God heals his back as well! He stood in complete shock that God would love him and heal him as he was with his girlfriend in Glen Falls. Since God is healing him he mentions his wrist is in a lot of pain from a fall, breaking his wrist while snowboarding. There is now metal in its place holding the wrist together, but it is causing him a lot of pain. The group shows him the sheet and he couldn't believe that clue was on there as well. He missed it when he looked at the sheet before. After praying for his wrist, the pain was gone and the popping and clicking disappeared as well.

After praying for the boyfriend, the group asked the girlfriend if she was open to prayer. After seeing her boyfriend get healed, she said she was definitely open to it. After praying for her knees and ankle, she said all the pain left and the popping that would always happen when she walked completely stopped. The group then prayed over anxiety and fear and she felt the peace of God come on her. To close, someone in the group had a word about past hurt/pain and a fear of them becoming like the person who hurt them. We shared that with God we are made new creations and transferred into his bloodline where we are no longer receiving anything from this world.

They both felt lighter and at peace and thanked us for our time with them. They said they would never be the same after that Jesus encounter.

"Can you search out the deep things of God? Can you find out the limits of the Almighty?" Job 11:7

REASON # 61

HE NEVER LETS
ME DOWN

It was 1999, and I was a young single mother of three teenage children. I had just purchased a $90,000 home for $54,000 in Kenmore NY, by the grace of God! His favor was upon me, as my family moved into this beautiful 1928, 2-story home, radiating with character and craftsmanship. It was the start of a new season for all of us. At the time, I was working for a lawyer handling class action law suits. I was one of 10 employees hired to help clients receive their settlements. As this specific pharmaceutical - Class Action suit was winding down, I noticed my fellow employees were all being let go one by one. I approached my boss and asked him if I was on that list too, because if I was I had a mortgage and three children to think about, and I would need to start looking for another job... ASAP! He assured me that I was one of his best employees, and that he had no intentions of letting me go.

God had shown me great favor while working for this man. I was able to witness to those around me about God's unfailing love and salvation. I even had the privilege of leading a co-worker to Christ. It was exciting to listen to her come to work with stories, almost daily, of God's faithfulness to her. She was blown away by the way God kept revealing Himself to her, and how He kept meeting her needs. I had been blessed beyond measure in working here.

But one Saturday afternoon the phone rang, and I got the call I thought I never would… It was my boss telling me he would have to let me go. He was very sorry, but he couldn't afford to keep me on any longer. He was very apologetic, and I assured Him that my God was bigger than these circumstances, and that I would be just fine. I never once felt alarmed. God's peace that surpasses all understanding just flooded me with assurance that He had this. God had never let me down before, so why would He start now!

One evening as I attended a dance practice at the church I attended, New Covenant Tabernacle in Tonawanda, one of my fellow dance team members asked where I was searching for work. She asked if I had a resume. I told her I didn't, so she offered to come to my house and help me put one together. She told me there was a company right around the corner from me called "The Talking Phone Book" that might be hiring. She was right! The next day I dropped off my resume, and within an hour I received a phone call for an interview. A few weeks later I was working for this great company. I made twice as much as I had previously been making! Again, God opened up the doors to witness. I handed out Bibles to my co-workers and spoke of my amazing God.

About six months had passed and I was still playing catch-up financially, from when I was laid off. Though I had money coming in for my current bills, it wasn't enough to pay off the 3 months back mortgage and other bills I had accumulated while out of work. Christmas was approaching, and I remember being honest with my kids and letting them know there would be no Christmas this year. They were just leaving for New Jersey with their dad to visit family for the holidays, and I was thankful there would be gifts waiting for them under the tree when they got there.

Meanwhile, I was in the process of looking for a new place to live for me and my family. We could no longer afford our beautiful home. But I knew God was aware of everything, and I trusted that He knew what He was doing. Everywhere I looked it just didn't feel right... it didn't feel like home. The home we had felt like home... and it was. God was working behind the scenes and I didn't even know it...

One afternoon, the day before Christmas, the phone rang. On the other end of the line was my former boss, who 9 months earlier had let me go. He told me he had been thinking about me, and how he left me in a financial bind. He said he never had the chance to give me the bonuses I deserved, and he wanted to make it up to me. We talked for a while, and he told me he had written me a check for $1500 and I should be receiving it in the mail any day. It was such a blessing and I couldn't believe he was thinking of me. We hung up and I called my kids to tell them the good news. But God wasn't finished yet. Again, the phone rang, and by now it was a few days after Christmas; it was my former boss again. He sounded genuinely concerned that he still didn't do enough for me. He point blankly asked me for the dollar amount of every outstanding bill I acquired while I was laid-off from work, and he wanted me to bring these bills to his office.

The next day I went to his office and laid every bill I had on his desk. He added them all up and with no hesitation he wrote me another check for $3500! Only God could have touched this man's heart. He was a business man and I'm sure he wasn't in the habit of looking back and making arrears to anyone. But God so touched his heart for me that it was as if he wasn't going to rest until he made out that check! Within 1 week I had received $5000 from this man, which not only saved me from having to sell my home, it was another testimony I could share with my children of God's faithfulness!

I knew my former boss was a Jewish man, but that didn't stop me from purchasing a Bible for him. I mailed it off to him with a card explaining how God used him to meet my needs, and that God wanted in return to bless him, by introducing him to his Messiah... Jesus Christ. Years later I bumped into this man while on lunch with some co-workers. We shared hellos and I could see in his smile that he had never forgotten me, and I had never forgotten him either. He was up in years, and I could only hope that he truly did meet his Messiah...

Mary Genovese

"The LORD will command the blessing on you in your storehouses and in all to which you set your hand, and He will bless you in the land which the LORD your God is giving you."
Deuteronomy 28:8

REASON # 62

HE IS ALWAYS
WITH US

This next testimony is amazing, but true....

It was nighttime, but I was fully awake lying in bed. At the time, I slept on a water bed. All of a sudden, I could sense someone in the room. Someone began to jump on the bed to the point I could hear the water swishing around, but I could not see anyone. I was so scared that I screamed out to God - What is this! What is this!

Then I heard an audible voice that said, "Just grab my hand!" I looked up and there was a hand. I had to really stretch my arm out to reach the hand. Once I grabbed His hand - everything went away. That day God taught me about a realm that I knew nothing of... the realm of darkness and spiritual warfare.

I was happy to include the above testimony because it reassures us that God misses nothing. He is with us when we rise up in the morning, as we walk in the way, and as we lie down at night. He never leaves our side. Be assured that you are never alone. Let us be reminded that the forces of darkness are no match for God. I too, have been confronted by this type of harassment, but in the same way this woman called out to God, I did too. And I had the same results... nothing was left in the room but me and God. If you find yourself in a place like this... cry out to God in the name of His Son Jesus... The name of all names! The name of Jesus is our weapon of warfare against a real enemy that not only wants to destroy us, but harass us. There is no reason to fear, because we are safe in the arms of God...

Kelley

"For God has not given us a spirit of fear, but of power and of love and of a sound mind." 2 Timothy 1:7

REASON # 63

HIS AMAZING GRACE

I t was the late 1980s and Morris Cerullo was hosting a crusade in Manhattan, NYC. It was also my first time serving as an altar worker. I attended the training sessions, handed out leaflets promoting the event, and was assigned a section of the amphitheater over which to pray for people and report testimonies. There was a heightened atmosphere of faith! I prayed earnestly for those seeking miracles and healing. In all the excitement. I had forgotten my own struggle of lower back pain, emanating from a large lump on my spine. Stretching and chiropractic adjustments had not relieved the pain, which could be quite debilitating most mornings, or climbing flights of stairs to my fourth floor classroom at the junior high school where I taught, in Brooklyn.

The crusade was spiritually powerful, with many, many testimonies of healing! Still soaring from the surge of faith I experienced during the crusade, a few days later while kneeling before the Lord in fervent prayer, I reached around to my lower back (more from habit than from pain), to feel the lump on by spine. To my amazement, it was gone! I ran my finger higher then lower, up and down my spine several times, to find the lump. There was no lump! No pain! No stiffness! No aching!!! I tried various movements which had previously been difficult. I could move with total ease! All symptoms had completely *disappeared!* I was completely healed!! Praise God! As I prayed to Him for healing for *others,* God was *healing me!* And I am overjoyed to tell you, more than 30 years later…my lower back has remained PAIN-FREE! No symptoms whatsoever!!! God is so loving and compassionate. So amazing and transcendent. He never ceases to amaze me!

Leslie

"But seek first the Kingdom of God and His righteousness, and all these things shall be added to you." Matthew 6:33

REASON # 64

HE KNOWS MY
PAIN

If you've never suffered from arthritis before, it would be hard for you to understand just how debilitating of a disease it is. I was plagued with Arthritis in my neck for twenty years and the daily pain made even the simple things in life difficult to enjoy. I had to take these huge pills every day just to be able to function without excruciating pain in my neck. Turning my head to drive was a huge ordeal without my pills. I could not be without my pills for a week or the pain would return if I tried to turn my neck to the right or to the left.

I was scheduled for surgery on another part of my body and I was told to stop taking my arthritis pills two weeks before surgery as the pills could cause severe complications. I didn't know how I was going to function without the pills. I thought maybe I could handle the pain associated with arthritis so I could have the surgery.

I stopped taking the pills and before the end of the first week the pain was unbelievable and unbearable. I literally couldn't move my neck in any direction and surgery was still one week away. I took all this into prayer and cried out to God that He would take away my pain. Through the tears I sensed God had touched me. It couldn't be true! Was the pain really gone! The Lord healed me instantly! 20 years of pain! I am so happy to tell you that I am free of taking those huge arthritic pills! All my arthritis is gone! By His stripes I am healed, and I am so grateful to our Lord.

GG

"Who Himself bore our sins in His own body on the tree, that we, having died to sins, might live for righteousness—by whose stripes you were healed.". 1 Peter 2:24

REASON # 65

HE BRINGS
ME JOY

Oftentimes we think of miracles as happening in an instant. We picture meetings of thousands where God supernaturally creates a missing limb, opens deaf ears, or sets free the oppressed in a moment . . . but sometimes miracles are a journey.

At least that was how it was with our miracle. We got married in 2009 and a year after marriage we were ready to have kids. We both loved kids and Veronica especially had an uncanny knack for being a "kid magnet" wherever we traveled. We would be walking down the street in a faraway place and kids would just gravitate to her. We were so excited at the thought of being parents.

On top of that we had a sense in our hearts that family and children was something God had for us. So we naturally expected that once we were ready we would be pregnant and soon have a growing family. Instead we spent the next 7 years walking through the difficult and sometimes dark valley of trying, waiting, and nothing happening. We went to doctors, had tests done and everything seemed normal but nothing was happening.

Unless you have experienced it, you can't imagine the pain, discouragement, and fear that can surround you. Daily, sometimes hourly we would have to speak to our souls and remember together that God had promised, and He was good. It was a long and hard season.

Finally in August of 2015 we felt to pursue adoption, to see if God might want to grow our family in that way. In John 14:18 Jesus expresses the Father's heart "I will not leave you orphans; I will come to you." We wondered if perhaps He was preparing us to be His heart of love extended to a child of His choosing. The next several months were filled with completing paperwork, meeting with lawyers and getting fingerprinted. Each day the reality of this precious opportunity became more and more real. We were excited at the possibility of welcoming a new life into our family and His love.

Again we were sure that this was the answer, and expected to soon have a child to love and welcome into our forever family. At the same time many couples in our ministry team were having kids, even other friends who had begun the adoption process with us, were holding a beautiful baby boy, but our arms remained empty.

Sometimes when we watched those around us with beautiful bouncing babies, the pain of waiting and the longing became almost unbearable. "Why God? Where are you? Are we ever going to experience this joy?" were all questions that swirled in our minds, and yet again and again we found our way back to the rock-solid truth that God was good, and that He was even working this out for His glory.

Over the next two and a half years we had several possible referrals for adoption, but in each case they didn't work out. So we kept waiting. Finally in November of 2017 we decided to make a video about this journey of waiting. We wanted to share with others who were also in the midst of the waiting what God had shown us of His love, goodness and faithfulness before the answer had come. We began making a testimony video (http://www.thejenksfamily.com/adoptionstory) sharing all God had done in the midst of this "waiting season," when suddenly we got a call that there was a birth mother who was due in about 6 weeks and was looking for a home to place her child for adoption. After all the waiting, possibilities and disappointments we didn't want to get our hopes up, but we prayed about it and tentatively set up a meeting with lawyers to discuss it. After the meeting, we felt to take the next step.

Suddenly we found out that our paperwork had somehow lapsed and we had to complete everything all over again! This was the same paperwork that had taken us months to fill out, and the birth mom was due in 6 weeks! That was when the Lord reminded us of a prophetic word we had gotten a few days before the call "The Lord says, he will make a way, where there seems to be no way. Just like I parted the Red Sea for Moses the obstacles in your way will be moved." We took heart and set to work completing everything. Remarkably what took us months the first time was completed in just two weeks, and on February 16 we welcomed a beautiful baby girl Abigail Eliezra Jenks into our home & our lives!

Abigail - "Father's Joy"
Eliezra (El-ee-ehzra) - "My God is my salvation"

The years of waiting, believing, and trusting for God to bring children to our family, have given way to euphoric joy and gratefulness to the Lord as we celebrated the arrival of this

precious promise. This journey of adoption has been one of the most difficult and beautiful experiences we've ever been through. Difficult because there were so many unknowns all along the way, but beautiful because God has worked so many miracles, and woven so many other stories wrapped up into this one testimony.

Even the sweet young nurse who cared for Abigail in the hospital and welcomed us into the nursery and presented Abigail to us for the first time was impacted by God's love. As we were preparing to leave the hospital she said to us, "The last several days I had been in a funk, then you and Abigail came into my life, and then all of a sudden everything made sense. She was meant to be in my life."

We were blown away! God was using Abigail, only two days old, to display His love to others. We saw this as a confirmation of this little one's destiny and calling to bring many to the Father.

These are just a few of the many little miracles that have already surrounded Abigail's arrival, and this new chapter in our family.

We hope that our story continues to encourage you in whatever you are believing for. One of the scriptures the Lord gave us as was John 11:40:

Jesus said to her, "Did I not say to you that if you would believe you would see the glory of God?"

Truly, this journey has taught us much about believing. All glory to our God and Father who has brought His promise to pass in our lives.

In many ways, the journey has just begun. . .

Stephen, Veronica & Abigail Jenks

(To see a video of this testimony and learn more visit thejenksfamily.com)

"For He who is mighty has done great things for me, and Holy is His name." Luke 1:49

REASON # 66

HE IS WITH US IN OUR SUFFERING

It's through the cross of Jesus Christ that we have been given new life. The cross reminds us that we are loved, and that Jesus too has suffered. The following testimony points to the power that the cross still holds today in comforting our broken hearts. Our hope is in nothing less than Jesus Christ our righteousness... My Dad was suffering so badly, because my Mother was suffering so badly in a nursing home. She had Alzheimer's and he started to get bitter because she lived her whole life for God and he couldn't understand why God would let her suffer like that. One evening while I was staying with my dad he said, "You need to go into the kitchen and look out the window!" Well, I did and I was in awesome wonder at what I saw. It was a massive milky-white cross in the sky, in the valley, in back of a neighbor's home. It was ethereal, and towering up into the sky... this wasn't man-made. It just hung from the heavens. This window was a window my dad looked out every evening... God knew... God was showing him that He had not left my mother's side. He was answering my dad's prayer that night reminding him of His presence. I will never forget it... how awesome is our God!

Amazed

"Surely He has borne our griefs and carried our sorrows."

Isaiah 53:4a

REASON # 67

HE IS FAITHFUL

Scripture exhorts us to give testimony to the wonderful works of God! "Give thanks to the Lord, call on His name; proclaim His deeds among the peoples."

This is the testimony of a faithful God, who in our valleys, gives us courage....

I was born with a heart murmur and, as decades passed, I developed aortic stenosis. The only remedy for this is surgery, and a replacement heart valve. The alternative? Eventual death! However, the surgery itself carries its own risks. I knew that day would finally come because I was exhibiting signs of heart failure: shortness of breath, fatigue, dizziness, nausea, etc. One day, I went to the cardiologist for an echo cardiogram and she informed me it was time. In a sense, I was relieved because I wanted my life back. The supernatural peace of the Lord enveloped me, I normally would have been anxious, but I knew God was with me.

The song, "No Longer Slaves (of fear)" By Bethel Music, kept resonating in my mind as it ministered to me daily. As I listened to this song...over and over...the peace of God surrounded me. People were astonished that I didn't show any concern for my impending surgery. God told me that I was "kept by His power" and I believed Him.

As the process began, I sought the prayers of friends and family. We prayed... Who would do the surgery? The hospital it would take place in? The surgical staff assisting the surgeon; ICU nurses and other staff caring for me, etcetera. And, of course, my restoration and full recovery. I didn't know any cardiac surgeons, so I presented my request to find the best one to the Lord. It wasn't long before I began to hear the same surgeon's name...over and over. This doctor had operated on relatives or friends of people I knew. He came highly recommended. I believed he was God's answer. Later, this was confirmed when I received a call from the hospital saying this was the surgeon assigned to me! When I met with him for my pre-operation consultation, I left his office in total peace.

And so, on December 28, 2017, I underwent open heart surgery. And God, true to His word blessed me with excellent, caring medical staff. My ICU nurse even turned out to be a friend of my niece. Despite the many blessings, as with any surgery, there were challenges I encountered, which tested my faith. One occurred on my first day in ICU. My heart was not functioning properly. I found myself connected to an external pacemaker to force my heart to beat properly. Four days after my surgery, I received a permanent pacemaker, which solved this issue.

After spending eight days in the hospital, I was discharged. This is when the true recovery process began. My stamina and appetite were very low; I had to build myself up again. But during this trying time, I experienced the love of the body of Christ. So many people sent cards, provided dinners, and visited me at the hospital.

When I came home, people offered to take me for brief walks in the mall and continued to pray for me on this journey. My husband was by my side throughout, every step of the way. However, it was also during this time when the enemy tried to destroy me through several health hurdles, and some difficulty breathing. He would whisper in my ear negative thoughts, "You're not going to make it!" or "You're not going to regain your health again." I returned twice to the hospital as an out-patient, for additional testing. I was so weak, fear started to grip me. Nevertheless, God assured me He did not bring me this far to abandon me. My greatest weapon against the enemy's attacks was the Word of God. I quoted the Word of God aloud, mainly Psalm 91: 9-10; 14-16 and Psalm 23.

Upon my last visit to the hospital, I was prescribed anxiety medication. Over time, staying in the Presence of God refocused me, giving me peace and hope again. As Christians, we need to be mindful that the enemy often attacks when we are in our most vulnerable state. Nevertheless, "God is our refuge and strength, a very present help in time of trouble." Although it can be very hard at times, we need to remember that we can trust Him.

Today, I am recovering nicely and enjoying very good health... Praise God! I learned so much through this ordeal. God has kept His word, and I have trusted Him every step of the way. No matter how bleak and hopeless life can appear, God is always in control!

Janet

"For He himself has said, I will never leave you nor forsake you."
Hebrews 13:5

REASON # 68

HE'S GOT MY
BACK

Several years ago when I was 11 years old I went fishing with my cousins. We went to our favorite fishing spot just a half mile from my house. The location was down a narrow road with a bridge resting over a small creek. We would fish on either side of the bridge depending on where the fish were biting that day. The width of this bridge was just wide enough for one car to pass through at a time, and my cousins and I would fish across from each other on this bridge.

It was a warm day and perfect for fishing. I had been waiting all night and all I could do was think about the fish I would catch. My cousins where on one side and I was on the other waiting to be the first to catch a fish. After some time my cousin yelled, "I got one!" immediately, without thinking I turned and began to run to the other side of the bridge. I still remember the sound of the car screeching and a flash of something in my eyes. As I looked I saw a car turned facing me. To this day I still can't remember what the driver said. They were shook-up and very upset that I darted out in front of their car. The road was narrow and I can't even imagined how the car swerved and spun to face me sideways on the bridge without running me over.

My heart was beating a million miles an hour and I know something different happened that day. The sounds and flashes were like a dream and yet very real. The best way to explain it is like having a slow motion dream where the world around you is moving and the images are blurred, moving a little out of sync with you sight. At the same time you hear loud sounds of tires skidding on the asphalt.

So, was it just luck that the car missed me? I can tell you I have been down to the old fishing spot several times since, and based on where my cousins where I and I was, I can't see how the car made it past us without striking someone. How the car did a 180, missed me, my cousins, and the bridge, is nothing but a miracle. I have since stopped trying to analyze what had happened. I do believe God has a plan for all of us and He changed my destiny that day. I also believe the day had a double Blessing. My mistake would have not only cost me my life, but also wrecked the life of the driver who had no chance of stopping.

I still have visions of that day almost 45 years later. It's a feeling of getting a second chance on life, and knowing that God had my back when I was unable to see what was ahead.

Tony

"The Glory of the Lord shall be your rear guard." Isaiah 58:8

REASON # 69

HE CONNECTS
US

God always keeps me in awe of the way He connects people's lives for their good and His purposes. There have been a multitude of incidences through which God proved His love and intervention in unique situations in the people who become part of our life's story.

From a young age my grandson, John J. Levulis, was preparing to be a soldier and leader. His dedication to his community in Eden and our country was very apparent. As an Eagle Scout project, he approached local businessmen in the area to obtain funds to erect a monument to Eden's veterans. Upon graduation from Eden High School, John received a full scholarship to Niagara University's R.O.T.C. program. After being commissioned to 2nd Lt. in 2014, John and his platoon were deployed to Afghanistan. The tour was successful and all of John's platoon came safely home. On a furlough home, John brought a few soldiers to enjoy a day at the Eden Corn Festival where they were introduced to some hometown veterans. While in route from Camp Drum, N. Y. to Fort Dix, N.J. in May 2015 for more training, the Humvee John was in was hit by a speeding car which caused the Humvee to crash into a tree. John and the driver were ejected, and both lost their lives. John was planning on being married in July and would have completed his tour in the Army that October. John's family and friends formed a foundation in his name to support students from Eden High School and Niagara University with scholarships to further their education. The foundation is funded by having a golf tournament in July, and a soccer tournament in the fall. In 2016, my son Paul, approached people he worked with who might be interested to become a part of this cause. A fellow worker, Corey, who Paul didn't know at that time, was interested in John's story and invited a few friends to participate. This past February 2018, I attended a home Bible Study group, and as each woman shared our lives, I discovered that Mary, the compiler of this book, was Corey's mother. Both of our son's now know each other and work at the Federal Prison in Batavia.

Being part of the Bible Study made it possible for me to support Mary's dream to go to Israel this year. Also, our meeting has given me this opportunity to share how God uses our connections in life to bless others. When we have a relationship with the Lord He sets aside us and our loved ones for His will to be done. In my personal life, God has connected certain people to me. Many have enriched me by the spiritual growth I have received from them. There were some who needed me to give more of myself. People who cross our path help us to grow in God's love and knowledge of why we were created... to be more like Jesus. God connects all things together for our good, the good of others, and God's Glory.

A Grateful Grandmother,
Dorothy Levulis

*"But as for me, I trust in You, O LORD; I say, "You are my God."
My times are in Your hands..." Psalm 31: 14, 15*

REASON # 70

HE LEADS ME

One evening as I was getting ready for church, I searched for a bracelet to wear and spotted a gold one that I hadn't worn in years. I put it on and rushed out the door. That evening, while I was greeting new visitors at the church, I met a young lady named Elaine. I had this feeling that her life had not been easy. In our brief conversation, she said a relative had invited her to the concert at the church that night.

During the concert, the Holy Spirit spoke to me and said, "Give Elaine your bracelet." I looked for her during the intermission, and when I spotted her I walked over and placed the Gold bracelet on her wrist and said, "God told me to give you this bracelet." She seemed puzzled by the unusual gesture, but thanked me as I walked away. The following Sunday, Elaine hugged me and cried as she poured out her heart to me. She said, "I have been a prostitute for most of my adult life, and people always took from me. No one has ever given me anything without expecting something in return."

This was truly a God-appointed moment. I am so thankful that I was obedient to the Holy Spirit's voice that evening. I later found out that Elaine was dying from AIDS. This gold bracelet was a gift unlike any other she had ever received before. It would have been easy to reason away God's prompting that evening, and if I hadn't followed through, Elaine would never have known how much God loved her. Her heart was now open to receive God's greater gift of love and salvation.

As the Holy Spirit speaks to us, let us be prepared to give our best gift to Him. It could be the very thing that prepares the heart of someone most precious in His sight.

Don and Andrea Troyer

"... inasmuch as you did it to one of the least of these My brethren, you did it to Me.' Matthew 25:40

REASON # 71

HIS WHISPERS
ARE POWERFUL

I was "Born again" at St. Catherine's Catholic Church (Life Church now) in West Seneca. I was a part of the Catholic Charismatic movement of the seventies. At that time, I attended a Charismatic Conference being held in Toronto. My husband and I went together, and while he was driving I had to lie down in the back seat of the car. I laid back in the backseat the way there because my back was in such pain.

On Saturday afternoon, there were several masses being said in the dorms at the college where we were being housed. We walked into one room and it didn't feel right, so we walked out. But the next room we entered, we stayed and attended mass there. At the end of the mass, a woman whispered something into the priest's ear. This was right after Communion. He then said he had a couple of "words of knowledge" for someone.... "This is for Mary... I love you, really love you, and I'm going to heal your back." I knew no one there, and I could hardly believe my ears. If my husband hadn't heard it also I would have thought I was hallucinating. I went into the restroom and couldn't stop crying. Within 6 months my back was completely healed. Praise the Lord! I had been to several doctors and hospitals with no results. God did this for me! Our God is soooo Good!

"Have mercy on me. O Lord, for I am weak; O Lord heal me, for my bones are troubled." Psalm 6:2

REASON # 72

HE GIVES US
STRATEGIES

For years my parents felt the Lord leading them to read tons of books on marriage. One day when they were praying they felt the Lord calling them to be "fishers of marriages" in Buffalo. A few weeks later a friend of theirs who led a ministry called "Marriage Ministry International" contacted them and told them God was calling them to translate bibles around the world and the Lord told them He wanted my parents to run the ministry. At the time, my parents were not involved in ministry, but they had heard the Lord tell them this Himself ahead of time so they stepped into it.

My parents would pray and God would give them a name and a church. Every time they would contact the church with the name it would always turn out to be either the pastor or some of the top leaders in the church. The people that the Lord would lead them to would be on the brink of divorce. Pastors told my parents "I'm not living with my wife, I'm living with another woman", etc. Every time God would miraculously restore their marriage and ignite a marriage ministry in the church to strengthen the marriages there. After my parents did this for years, one time in a meeting this woman said, "I know who you guys are!" After the meeting was over she came up to my parents and told them "I used to be a witch, but today I am a

Christian. We would do séances against pastor's marriages in the region so they would end up in divorce. People would consider the leaders in their church Hippocrates and leave the church. Every time we were close, something would block us. Then we did a séance on what was blocking us and we got your families name and started doing séances". If you get anything from this story you should pray for the leaders in your church because you never know the full extent of what is going on in the spirit and what attacks are coming against them.

Brendan

"Brethren, pray for us." 1 Thessalonians 5:25

Whew this is an eye opener for me. Please take a moment and pray for your pastors and leaders. It is *our* weapon of warfare...

Dear Lord,
You know the importance of family, and the power of influence. Show Yourself strong on behalf of our Pastors and leaders today! You desire that they succeed and You desire that they bear fruit, so I ask that You strengthen and equip _____ (our Pastors and leaders) to fight the good fight, finish the race, and keep the faith. Place righteousness and truth in their hearts and minds. Warn them of enemy attack. Bring every evil word spoken against them to naught. Cut off the enemies lies, curses, and distractions. Let no weapon formed against our Pastors and leaders prosper. Keep them from temptation and deliver them from all evil. Protect their families, and keep the family unit as one; having no division. I bless our Pastors and leaders with favor and goodness. With prosperity and soundness. May they be blessed as they come, and blessed as they go. May they wear a radiant countenance all the days of their lives! May they be bold, and proclaim the "good news" of the love of Jesus Christ and His salvation, to every lost and dying soul. AMEN

REASON # 73

HE HEALS ME
TIME AND AGAIN

Have you ever experienced Vertigo? That feeling when the room is spinning at a hundred miles an hour or you're on a merry-go-round and can't get off? Well, imagine living with that feeling every day. Not a pleasant thought, right? Sadly, many people suffer with Vertigo for a long time, as was the case with this writer. Thank God, we have a healer!

For several years, I suffered with Vertigo, the feeling that the world is spinning out of control and you can't make it stop. There are several causes of Vertigo. According to my doctors, the type I experienced, BPPV – Benign Paroxysmal Positional Vertigo - was most likely caused by a fall. Following that fall, calcium particles broke away, clustering together, then crystalizing in my inner ear. This caused serious irritation to the tiny circular canals which controlled my balance. Doctors tried to treat me, by moving my head quickly, in an attempt to shake the crystals apart. Sometimes, this would help for a few weeks, only for the symptoms to return with a vengeance. They tried but could not help me.

If you've ever experienced Vertigo yourself, or even a simple bout of imbalance, then I'm sure you can understand why it's such a horrible condition. The symptoms are often so severe, it actually keeps you from leading a normal life. You can't drive a car or even walk straight. Even the simple act of turning over in bed can be an ordeal, as the room and bed seem to spin uncontrollably. Dizziness and nausea are the worst symptoms. The intense nausea Vertigo produces is likened to sea sickness - no exaggeration. At times, it was literally debilitating.

One day, I asked for prayer for deliverance. The Lord met me there and healed me! And it has never come back, for which I am eternally thankful. Praise God, He is our healer!

Gail B.

"For You created my inmost being; You knit me together in my mother's womb." Psalm 139:13

Dear Friend, are you suffering with a health condition? Have you tried everything with no relief? Why not ask the Great Physician to heal you? He knows your body from the inside out and exactly what you need. Pray to the God who created you...who knows you best. He is in the miracle-working business!

REASON # 74

HE DOESN'T LET
GO OF ME

On Sunday, 9/22/13, my family and I went on a family trip to West Virginia. We were going whitewater river rafting on the Gauley River. The Gauley River only runs in the fall after they release the dam. Little did we know they also had flooding the prior week. This made the river very strong. It normally runs at 2500-2800 cubic feet per second. On 9/22/13 it was running at 5500!! I had everyone praying for us on our trip, I also prayed that if the trip was unsafe, "Lord cancel this trip and give the guides wisdom." We were scheduled to do the upper Gauley River, but that was canceled due to hazardous conditions, so we were rescheduled for the lower Gauley.

We had the trip leader Shannon as our guide. Shannon had guided rafting trips in the biggest white water in Africa and New Zealand. We went through the first half of the trip just great! It was like being on a roller coaster on the water. After lunch, we entered into the second half of the trip. Shannon explained this half would be more intense, and to listen and follow directions very carefully. We entered in. The water was peaceful, it didn't look like we were about to go through double class 5 rapids. As we entered, our boat hit a rock, I flipped backwards, hanging upside down; my feet still wedged in the boat. Then we hit another Rock, and I flipped out of the boat! The guide Shannon, my husband Dan, my middle daughter Amanda and 3 others from another family all fell out. My eldest daughter Rhiannon and my youngest daughter Ashley remained in the boat. Everyone made it back to the boat except Shannon, the father of the other family, and myself. I was swept away so fast, the river water was too powerful. I was praying and asking the Lord for help and wisdom. The boat was stuck on an eddy, we were the first boat with no other boats where I was. I had only one thing... to trust the Lord! The Lord was the only one who could help me. As I gasped for air while the waves were crashing over me, I wasn't able to get air or catch my breath. I was swept under the water, swirling and tumbling, doing somersaults in the waves until I landed under a huge undercut rock.

The force of the water was pinning me. I kicked, pushed and prodded trying to free myself to no avail! Finally, I gave up in frustration and looked up and said, Lord, you know that people usually do not survive this, but Jesus get me out of here!! As soon as I said this the power of God hit me in my stomach and I flew backwards. My fanny was stuck in the hole in the rock just like the old cartoon characters would get stuck in the fence, then all of a sudden my whole body went flat, my head touched my toes, I was completely bent in half. Then I was sucked through the rock. Normally, after a flood, all of those holes are filled with debris, but nothing touched me. I flew through the rock out the other side, then swirled and twirled to the top of the river. I lifted my head and saw 2 silver boats, I tried yelling for help, but without air there is no vocal projection. Then I lost consciousness. I had been under the water for a little over 3 minutes. While I was under, my family had quite the journey down the river without their guide Shannon. They had the guidance of the Lord. They made it down the river before I did and had pulled over to wait for assistance. When they saw my life vest and then me, my daughters screamed! My face was white as a sheet, my lips were blue and my eyes completely red. They thought I had passed away. My husband Dan felt an urgent unction to go in after me and he did. There were lots of rocks in the river but you couldn't see them because they were covered by the high water. He dove in head first, flying over them, not hitting any rocks. He landed right in front of me and called my name. Immediately I opened my eyes still trying to yell for help. Then the other boats came and pulled us to safety. We parked on the side of the river for 45 minutes. I was praying and the Lord was faithful to restore my air, color and remove the redness from my eyes. Then we paddled down one more rapid to the evacuation point. I was assisted out of the boat and walked up a ravine only stopping once to catch my breath. Then we reached the RR tracks just as the nurse arrived. Her name was Kathy from Amherst NY, which is in the Buffalo NY area. She took my vitals and couldn't believe my vitals were near perfect. Then we started walking to meet the Ranger. I walked 2 miles without any human assistance, and another 1/2 mile across the bridge to meet the Ranger!

When everyone else returned from the trip, no one could believe I was the one pulled from the river that day. I didn't have any affects from the incident and didn't receive any medical treatment. Just the grace, mercy and faithfulness of the Lord I survived. I was able to share Jesus with everyone on the trip! Jesus Saves Hallelujah. Amen

Patty Drzymala

"Now I know that the Lord saves His anointed; He will answer him from His Holy Heaven with the saving strength of His right hand." Psalm 20:6

To watch the Youtube video of this dramatic moment caught on video go to: https://youtu.be/UVYiXoglw5g

REASON # 75

HE IS AWARE OF
EVERYTHING

This next story is a reminder that nothing takes God by surprise... as I listened to a friend recount a vision she had a week before September 11 2001, I was glued to her words. She foresaw in a vision, the chilling account of one of the worst days in American history. She described in her vision the towers, the planes, the smoke and the people running. I was stunned that God revealed this to her before it happened. But what left me speechless was what I heard next... the woman next to her said "I had a dream about 9/11 too! I couldn't believe my ears! She said in her dream the towers were represented by two tall trees that stood towering above all the rest in the forest. She said, "all of a sudden they came crashing down and smoke covered the forest, people began running out from the smoke in fear and panic." As I listened to these women speak I thought about why God reveals things to us in the first place. My answer would be to *pray*. We may not always understand what a dream or vision may mean, but if we've been given a glimpse into the future it's for a reason. My friend said she knows better now to pray even if she doesn't understand.   Gail & Kelley

"Hear my prayers O God; Give ear to the words of my mouth."
Psalm 54:2

REASON # 76

HE WEAVES US
INTO A
TAPESTRY

My life has been a tapestry of vivid colors. Many beautiful and some not so beautiful, but each thread individually woven together by God to form the person I am today. Even now, God continues to take my life with all of its ups and downs and create for Himself a masterpiece. Just a few weeks ago someone prophesied to me "God called you as a child." In my heart of hearts somehow, I always knew that. I was the only child of parents who waited seven years for me to be born. I had an Italian Catholic mother who prayed every day that God would send her a blonde haired, blue-eyed baby girl. The miracle is not so much that I was born, the miracle is that my parents are both Sicilian with dark hair and dark eyes. But, one day God answered my mother's prayer as she prayed the Stations of the Cross on one of the Catholic holy days at a church with an outside grotto. I went back to visit that church many years later and there's a stone placed in a garden on which is written *Jeremiah 1:5 "Before I formed you in the womb I knew you; Before you were born I sanctified you; I ordained you a prophet to the nations."* God had always had a plan and purpose, and always desired that I would be used by Him to teach the body of Christ His Word.

Being an only child of parents who adored me the first 16 years of my life were nearly perfect and then one day my dad, who I loved more than anyone, had heart attack and passed from this world. My mother continued to love and support me. She became my best friend, my counselor my comforter everything a mother could be in so much more.

Unfortunately, the next phase of my life was not so happy. Except for my beautiful daughter, the threads in the tapestry were mostly gray. Being married to a drug user and an alcoholic for over 20 years was the antithesis of my youth. Every day was a struggle, so it was a little hard in those days to believe that I had a future and a hope.

One day in the most dire of circumstances everything changed. I was in the hospital with an infection raging through my body. Through the pain I heard the doctor in the hallway saying He needed to speak with a family member. "This girl is going to die." I was a little shocked at his words. My marriage was over, and I was soon to be a single mom and I remember thinking, I'm only 38 years old am I really going to die? As soon as I had that thought it was like instantly, the presence of the Lord filled the room in a way I had never experienced before. I always had a God consciousness and a love for God, but this was different. This voice spoke not into my ears but into my heart and He said, "you're not going to die, and your life will never be the same." Almost immediately the doctor who announced that I was going to die came back in the room with hope in his eyes. He said he thought he had a plan to save my life. Later I told him the plan was not his but God's! Two surgeries later I left the hospital with a word in my heart from God, and no idea where the journey was going to take me. I struggled on that journey for about a year searching, wanting to find the God that was in that room with me. One morning I cried out to God and said, I don't know where you are. I can't find you please send me someone to tell me where You are. I then began my day as a hairdresser. Later that morning I had an appointment to give a girl a perm, I had no idea that she was going to be the one not only to tell me where God was, but what He was about to do with the rest of my life. She was like an angel sent from God into my life for such a time as this. She prayed for me, encourage me, taught me the Word, and prophesied great and mighty things for my life.

As you can tell, my life had been a lesson in contrast, very good and very bad. So, my question was how was God going to be God in the life of someone who went from being treated like a treasure to treated like trash? The answer was, *"not by might nor by power, but by His spirit."*

The next miracle in my life was that I received a full scholarship to Houghton College, twenty-five years after I graduated from high school, I received a Bachelor of Arts Degree in Biblical Studies and Counseling Psychology. Upon graduation, again came the question what now? Looking back, I realize how heavy God's hand was on my life. At our last chapel service, all of the graduates were asked, "What is your dream for the future?" My answer was, "To be an integral part of a World-Wide Ministry." Little did I know God would connect me to the dreamer of all dreamers Tommy

Reid! Bishop Tommy taught me how to dream and opened doors and introduced me to people that in my wildest dreams I would never have imagined meeting. I was ordained to ministry by him and I have credentials with The Assemblies of God.

Shortly after graduation, I was offered the position of Dean of students at Buffalo school of the Bible. I served in that ministry for 10 years and the one thing I knew was that I was called to teach the Word. When the school was given to another educational institution I became the director of pastoral care. In that role I have had the opportunity touch lives in the best of times, and in the worst of times. As I pass the 30-year anniversary of my tenure as an Associate Pastor at The Tabernacle, I have decided to semi-retire. I'm looking toward the future and believing the Lord to open even more doors. My prayer is that through Him I will not retire but Re-Fire.

Pastor Jo Ann Angelo

"A Father to the Fatherless, a defender of widows, is God in His holy habitation." Psalm 68:5

REASON # 77

HE TEACHES ME
HIS WAYS

In 1987 I was hit by a car driving a moped. I was in a coma for over a week with a closed head injury. My "Glasgow Coma Score" was a 5, with a minimum being 3 and the maximum being 15, I was very close to being brain dead. It took me about 10 years to recover. Today, I manage over 12 million dollars as an investment adviser! I have always believed it was a miracle from God that I was still alive. The Holy Spirit helped me understand that the accident was a blessing in disguise from God. I know this now because of what happened next.

I have been an avid hunter for almost 40 years. I am extremely agile climbing trees and getting into my tree stands. I never even slipped or lost my balance climbing or sitting in my stand, in the 1000 hours I've racked up over the years. But, 2 years ago, November 2015, I slipped and fell out of my tree stand. I later took a measuring tape and calculated that my fall was 19 feet to the ground. When I started to fall, I yelled out "LORD!" Pleading for God's help.

The first thing to hit the ground was my forehead, leaving a gash about 3" across my forehead. I heard around 10 loud crunches as I laid semi-conscious on the ground. My only thought was "how will I take my son to tennis practice in a wheel chair." I knew I broke my neck. After about 10 days of soreness I have never felt or had an issue with my spine and neck. Ten months later at my physical, my doctor sent me to a concussion specialist, and he said I have no issues either! The Spirit of God has now equipped me to preach at a church of a close Pastor friend of mine, on the Power of God! The later accident was clearly a miracle and the former, a blessing that strengthened me, and drew me close to God. I now know the difference in how God moves in our lives as He teaches us every step of the way!

James

"So teach us to number our days, that we may gain a heart of wisdom." Psalm 90:12

REASON # 78

HE HAS A HEART FOR THE HOMELESS

Below is a testimony of the Lord moving in an amazing way at Hearts for the Homeless. Our Lord has always been faithful in our times of need at the ministry. Below is just one of the many, many times the Lord made a way when we saw no way.

In the very early years of the ministry, we only had one computer, which I needed desperately for doing all the administrative work for Hearts. One day the computer simply died!

Hearts didn't have a lot of money but we took the computer in to be repaired. The repair man called me and said it would take $250.00 to fix it and to me in those days it was like he was saying $1000.00! I said I would have to talk to my husband, Ron about whether we had the finances to fix it, or if we should just get a new one. When I talked to Ron, he said we could not afford a new one and he told me to tell the man to fix the one we had.

I hung up the phone and told our staff that we all needed to be praying, and that we needed $250.00 to fix our computer. We didn't even have that extra in the budget. Within ½ hour after my phone conversation with the repair man, one of our staff members told me there was two of our soup kitchen volunteers (a husband and wife) at the ministry center and they wanted to talk to me. I came upstairs and welcomed them and asked why they were here, it wasn't their day to go out with the soup kitchen.

They proceeded to tell me they had a check for me from a small inheritance they had received and felt to give a part of it to Hearts. When I opened the envelope, it was $250.00! I was astounded and told them about the call I had received about our computer not ½ hour before. I said they needed to come downstairs for the staff to see the check and to see how quickly the Lord can move. Then later that day the repair man called me back and said he had over quoted me the repair price that it was only $150.00! I will never forget how the Lord moved and am so grateful to give testimony to this so many times over the years so HE ALONE CAN BE GLORIFIED. The blood of the Lamb and the word of our testimony, no one can dispute this. He has been so faithful these many years to show Himself so real in our times of need at Hearts.

Ron and Peg Calandra

"Is this not the fast I have chosen…"   Isaiah 58:6-12

To learn more about supporting this local ministry you can find them on Facebook or contact them directly: (716) 876-7346

Hearts for the Homeless
890 Tonawanda Street
Buffalo NY 14207

REASON # 79

HIS WAY IS THE
ONLY WAY

Music is my Life...

I was saved the day I realized the song "I Did It My Way" was completely wrong!

John K. Valan

"For as the heavens are higher than the earth, so are My ways higher than your ways, and My thoughts higher than your thoughts, says the Lord." Isaiah 55:9

REASON # 80

HIS PLACES THE
ORPHAN IN
FAMILIES

Things don't always go as planned in our lives, but it's the perfect plan in God's eyes... Our testimony involves a change of heart, a step of faith, God's provision, changing directions, and finally a fulfilled dream!

Early in our marriage all our efforts to start a family resulted in disappointment at every turn. After a few years of frustration our attention and focus gradually started to shift to the possibility of pursuing an adoption. As we discussed the process and began to explore various options we always seemed to come back to foreign adoptions. At this time a local adoption was not a sure thing and was over a two year process. We then started to research foreign adoptions. Several countries had programs and we started to gather information from different agencies. China appeared to be an open door, but the cost was very high and was on the other side of the world. It did not seem like a viable option.

We began to pray and as the days passed, it seemed like we were being drawn in that direction. It was interesting and probably not a coincidence that everywhere we went we were suddenly surrounded by cute Chinese children, whether it be the mall, at a restaurant or at a park. We started to think that maybe God was telling us something. God was slowly but surely changing our hearts and pointed us in a new direction. Then we started to receive confirmations from others, from friends, prayer groups and our Pastor. It sure seemed like the light was green for us to go forward. But the one stumbling block in our way was the cost.

However, if this was really God, He would make a way. So in faith, we decided to take baby steps with a Home Study, then the voluminous application process, record searches, financial statements, passports, health records and recommendations. As we moved steadily through the process, we started to receive financial help from unexpected sources and in many different ways. Relatives, friends and even my company contributed, suddenly what once seemed out of reach now seemed possible. It's wonderful to see how God works. A simple favor that once touched a person's heart in a time of sorrow, turned into a large check at just the right time.

By this time the excitement was building and there was no turning back. Then came the day we finally received a photo in the mail. It was a single photo of a little Chinese baby. She had been selected for us and we needed to make a decision. The baby girl had been left at the doorway of a police station, with no note and no date of birth. We examined every inch of that photo, with our hearts racing. We had a mixture of excitement and some anxiety. Do we really have to make a decision based on one photo? The baby was maybe 7 months old.

We showed the picture to family and received our confirmation. But when we called to say yes, we were told that we took too long and she might not be available. Our heats sunk as we pleaded to check her status. The call came back that she was still available and we cried with tears of joy thanking the Lord.

We now needed to make our travel plans. But two days later there was a surprise all office meeting at work. Our office would be closing and all jobs would be eliminated in two months. That was a devastating blow. Not only would we be losing a job, but possibly the baby as well. The timing could not have been worse. Did we miss God? How could this happen so expectantly?

Well, God is always in control and we had seen His hand at work in every step of this process. We had to make a decision and decided to go forward with the adoption plans. It was another step of faith and a short time later we received God's provision. The Lord gave us an idea to write a proposal and an outline for a remote worker position. The paper was submitted to the company. After further discussions with the company leadership and God's favor, we received a miracle. The company created its first remote worker position and a short time later I was retained to work at home with several other employees. During this time, one hundred fifty people lost their jobs and three were saved.

We made the trip to China and adopted Danielle, who recently graduated from college and obtained her first Art Teacher job. We also adopted our son Michael from Guatemala,

who is now in high school. He was another miracle, as God again provided every penny of the cost. This adoption also involved a journey with new lessons to be learned. With Danielle, God took us on a journey of change, faith and finally provision. It wasn't always an easy journey, but the lesson involved trust. Was God really going to come through for us and can we really trust Him even though we couldn't see the finish line? There were sleepless nights and tears, but God never fails and His blessings are new every morning.

Bob & Nancy Bruch

"Bless the Lord, O my soul, and forget not all His benefits"
Psalm 103:2

REASON # 81

HE PUTS WIND IN MY SAILS

In April of 2015, after a week of great ministry success, I got the shock of my life. I had a procedure done, and went back to my Doctor for follow up. Instead of saying what I expected him to say, "Everything is fine, see you in a couple years," he said, "You have prostate cancer."

I was shocked. I couldn't even process that, and then I had to go home and tell my wife. As a pastor, I've walked with a lot of people through a cancer diagnosis, but experiencing it for myself definitely changed me. I had to deal with thoughts of fear and all the "what if" questions.

John Maxwell says: "The pessimist complains about the wind. The optimist expects it to change. The leader adjusts the sails." After the initial shock wore off for me, I began to adjust my sails!

I had to learn all over again how <u>not</u> to give into fear and discouragement. I had to face once again what makes the difference between victory and defeat in our lives. This was a fight on a more personal level than I had ever experienced before. After multiple MRIs and tests, the doctors gave me the option to either get treatment immediately or to wait. After several more opinions, I decided I would wait the six months.

228

I had to remind myself that God loves me and that I can trust Him in every area of my life. I remembered all the blessings God had already given me in the past. I remembered that His promises are for me.

I took God at His Word, the living Word which is Jesus, the written word, the Bible and the prophetic Word, prophecy and words of encouragement. Many Believers gave me encouraging words, prophetic words, and Scripture to meditate on. Doctors don't have all the answers, but the Word of God is entirely and always true. I chose to have a positive mindset. It's not our circumstances that make us negative. It's our attitude towards the circumstances that make us negative. Positive people have made up their minds to enjoy life. They see possibilities not problems. They are thankful for what they have, not ungrateful for what they don't have. They know God is in control, and nothing happens without His permission. You have to choose every day to be positive.

In October of 2015, six months after I had been diagnosed, I received the report that I was completely cancer free. How did that happen? I don't know the exact moment when I was healed, but I felt even as early as April and May that God had healed me. Remember, I had received several diagnoses from doctors and MRI's that the cancer was there. I had no treatments. The Lord healed me! The doctors, nurses and radiologists were all amazed! *The Lord makes everything beautiful in its time* (Ecclesiastes 3:11).

I still get checked every 6 months. Recently I've had a lot of people contact me when they struggle with a bad diagnosis. Not just people in our church, but pastors and leaders from other areas. At first I was surprised, but then I realized that it is because I have a testimony. If Jesus can do this for me, He can do it for you and for others.

Pastor Ron Burgio

"Worship God! For the testimony of Jesus is the spirit of prophecy" Revelation 19:10b

REASON # 82

HE MAKES ALL
THINGS NEW

One night, some years ago, I was experiencing bad pain in my chest and back. I spent the evening sitting up in a recliner. My friend next door was concerned for me and said she was going to take me to the emergency room at the local hospital. So off we went. A long story short, they sent me to get a CAT scan to figure out where the pain was coming from. It turned out I had Pancreatitis, and they kept me one more night for observation. The next day a doctor came to me at my bedside and said "if you need your gallbladder out here is my card."

I really did not hear anything about my gallbladder from my doctor, even though I knew all of those organs work together. I left the hospital that day and when I got home I called my prayer warrior sister Jane who was in Kenya. We stormed the heavens for my healing, that I would not have to undergo any surgery...

That winter, I received in the mail a surgery date to remove my gallbladder on January 5th... "Oh, no" I said to myself. I called the hospital immediately and got the doctor on the phone, and told him I did not want surgery. He asked me how I felt, and I let him know that I hadn't felt pain for a while now. He agreed that surgery would not be necessary. NO Operation!

Well, time passed, probably about 3 years, and my doctor wanted me to have a liver scan because some test results didn't come back normal. I went to my appointment for the scan, and the technician said "I don't understand this. I have a record of your old gallbladder and it was very diseased looking - like an elderly person's organ. However, she said, your existing gallbladder looks brand new! How could this happen??" Well, I proceeded to tell her it was a miracle that happened three years before!!

Our God is Awesome and mighty! "Praise to His Holy Name"

Blessed

"He does great things too marvelous to understand. He performs countless miracles." Job 5:9

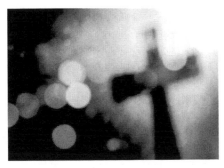

REASON # 83

HE HAS FASHIONED AND FORMED ME

M y Dad was an amazing man – kind, gentle, loving and a friend to all. To know him was to love him. I'm not sure what everyone loved more about him - his big heart, great sense of humor or the fact that he was always ready, willing and able to help those in need. When he passed away, the funeral home was standing-room only. As a matter of fact, a local Policeman who escorted Dad's funeral procession asked if a "local celebrity" passed away. He said he hadn't seen as long a procession (8-car police escort) since his military comrade, a decorated war hero, died during Vietnam. Indeed, to say my Dad was "one of a kind" wouldn't even begin to describe the kind of man he was.

Due to an unavoidable injury incurred at birth, my Father was handicapped his entire life. In order to save my Dad and Grandmother and remove him from the birth canal, the doctor delivering him had no choice but to break his left arm, at the elbow. As was common then, my Grandmother delivered at home. Back in 1932, most women still gave birth naturally, at home. Cesarean Sections were not common and mainly done in hospitals, in a sterile setting. Following his birth, doctors tried to set my Father's arm a few times but it didn't work. Hence, my Father lived with his left arm and hand permanently disabled, about half of its normal size and permanently bent at the elbow. His hand was permanently set in a fist. Dad would have to use his right hand to open his fingers on his left hand.

Despite this disability, Dad worked hard all his life. As a boy and teen, he helped his elderly Grandfather work his farm. Following his Grandfather's death, Dad worked "on-the-books". One evening after work, at age 22, he visited Woodlawn Diner on Route 5 in Woodlawn, NY, where he met my Mother, who served him. Soon after, they began dating. My Mother would often joke, "The night we met, I served him coffee. And I've been serving him coffee ever since!"

That cup of coffee led to marriage, then five children – two sons and three daughters - with me as the youngest. Dad always worked very hard to support our large family - often around-the-clock - at two different jobs. He never complained, though. A mechanic by trade, he'd also take odd jobs repairing vehicles periodically (in-between jobs). And he did all this with just one arm and hand! That arm was amazingly strong, too. So strong, I once saw Dad lift a man off the ground by his shirt collar! That man had sold our family a lemon car! Let me tell you, after days of ignoring Dad's phone calls and requesting his money back, that man reimbursed him instantly! About three years old at the time, I watched in disbelief, through a borrowed car's window because it was so out of character for my "gentle giant". But Dad always took care of us and protected us, so he did what he had to do, in order to purchase another reliable vehicle for our family.

My Dad was truly an amazing man – in thought, word and deed. He was an amazing father – gentle and fun but tough-as-nails when he had to be. He was my rock growing up, especially after he was hurt on the job and forced to retire early. After my Mother, who'd always been a stay-at-home Mom, went to work to supplement the household income, Dad became my full-time parent. During my teens, Dad was patient and understanding father, a comical "taxi" driver" to my many school and extra-curricular activities. And Dad always watched out for me. I had more (platonic) guy friends than girlfriends in high school and he'd sometimes screen my calls to ensure they were "just friends". Haha! I hated it at the time. But now that I look back, I realize how fortunate I truly was to have an earthly Father who cared so much about me. He stayed loving and caring after I married and moved out, too. He'd often call to check on me or pop in for coffee. He was my rock, the one person I could always rely on, no matter what.

But one day, all that came to a screeching halt! My world came crashing down when Dad passed away suddenly from a heart attack. I was devastated! It felt like my whole world literally imploded on me. I wandered through the dense fog of confusion and shock, aimlessly. Until I fell into the deep abyss of depression and became despondent. My three daughters were young then – ages 6, 4 and 2 years. I functioned daily (for them) but inside I was barely breathing. Friends and family told me they were very worried about me but I told them I was "fine". Which wasn't true at all. But I didn't realize at that time how far "gone" I truly was. My (then) husband tried to be supportive but didn't really know how to help me. One night, as I was sobbing uncontrollably, he reached out to me and we made love. Later that night, I had the most vivid dream I have ever had in my entire life! I saw my Dad standing there with an aura around him, a soft glow. No audible words passed between us, yet we definitely communicated, spirit to spirit. I asked him, "Dad, what are you doing here?" and he replied, "Karen, I came to say goodbye." It had been several months since he'd passed and I was confused. He continued, "I didn't want to leave you the way I did." I told him how much I missed him and how life wasn't the same without him. I don't remember communicating to him that I would rather be with him, in Heaven, but somehow he knew. He assured me, "God sent me to tell you that you are going to have a Son." To which I replied, "I can't, Dad. He doesn't want more children. He said three is enough. Don't you remember?" To which my Dad replied, "You *will* have a son because God knows you need him now. He will be a lot like me and he will give you the will to live again. Your daughters need you back." After he said this, he reach out and embraced me. A warm hug…my Daddy's hug. But something was very different about this embrace – he was holding me with *two full-length arms* versus one! And as he embraced me I felt a warmth radiate throughout my entire being, as a bright light surrounded us. Indeed, my entire being was tingling and I felt a light shock in my womb, like a million tiny butterflies, all at once.

Then, poof! Just as suddenly as Dad had appeared, he was gone. I remember sitting bolt upright in bed and looking around me, very disoriented. I literally felt like I'd just had an out-of-body

236

experience! Then, my husband woke up and looked at me concerned, "What's wrong? Are you all right?" I replied, "Yes, I'm fine. I just saw my father and he told me we're going to have a baby." His reply, "No, we're not. Go back to sleep; you were just dreaming." But I knew it was true. The next day, I called my eldest sister, with whom I'd always been close, and told her about my "dream". She didn't believe me, either, and said it was just a dream brought on by grief. But, just two weeks later, I took an early pregnancy test. Sure enough, it was positive! You can imagine my husband's and sister's astonishment when I told them I was expecting! They just looked at me, shocked! From the night of that dream on, everything was different! I was finally at peace after my Dad's passing. My whole outlook on life changed again! I now had a new life inside me, something exciting to look forward to, and I realized I had to start taking better care of myself again, for *all* of us. I started to laugh again and my joy returned! People said I was a completely different person. And I was. Praise God!! ☺ He had delivered me from Depression!!! Nine months later, I gave birth to a bouncing baby boy. My Son was born with my father's jet-black hair and hazel eyes. He is now almost 22 years old and his hair has lightened to a medium brown. But he still has my Dad's sparkling hazel eyes and he really does resemble my Dad in appearance and personality. Although he never knew his Grandfather, my Son has my father's name, Douglas, as his middle name. Christian definition of Douglas - "Seeker of Light." I will never forget that dream because it was much more than a dream. It was a prophetic vision! I *know* Dad received his healing in Heaven because he hugged me with *2 arms!* And I will never, ever forget the bright light that surrounded us, nor the shock in my womb. Because I know, at that very moment, the Holy Spirit placed my Son within my womb. No one will ever tell me differently because *I know that I know* it was real! It was too surreal *not* to be real. And the evidence is alive and walking today! Since then, Scientific studies have confirmed that, at the point of conception, there is a spontaneous burst of light – a spark – in the womb! I truly believe this is when the Spirit of the unborn child enters the womb, as my Son did that night, when God spoke and said, "Boom! Let it be." Our God is so amazing! Always creating miracles…in the most miraculous ways!!!

Karen Weaver

"For You formed my inward parts; You covered me in my mother's womb." Psalm 139:13

REASON # 84

HE IS MY
STRENGTH

Many years ago, a sudden snow storm overtook our city of Buffalo. It affected only certain isolated areas of the city, and was referred to as the "October Storm." Twenty-four inches of heavy, wet snow fell over two days. Our area was declared a 'major disaster' by the President, and some people even qualified for assistance through FEMA. My toddler and I were spending an extended weekend at home alone while my husband was away on a business trip, out-of-state in sunny Florida, approximately 1000 miles away, completely unaware of what was going on back at the homestead.

At the time, it seemed nobody expected such a severe storm to come upon our city, even the local weather personnel hadn't prepared us. It was quite a surprise, and not a pleasant one for many of the people it affected. I had recently learned the truth about salvation, while attending an evangelical Baptist church. Bible study and prayer were highly encouraged by my pastors and teachers there, so looking back I believe I was being prepared spiritually for such a crisis as this. At the time, I had very little physical energy due to recently overcoming a rather debilitating illness, working part-time outside the home, and trying to do my best to take care of our toddler while my husband worked hard to establish his business. Looking back, I thank God I remembered the Word I was taught, and at least I had a mustard seed of faith in Christ. At the time, I had only an antiquated emergency cell phone that I rarely used. The land-line phone and power lines were down, and it needed to be charged frequently. I wasn't sure how long it would last. We had a fireplace that my husband usually tended to, but that was somewhat of a mystery to me. Even though this storm was sudden, our Northeastern, Lakeside city is no stranger to storms. I often leaned on my husband in times like these. He was usually diligent in protecting and providing for our little family's needs by making sure our driveway was plowed, and that we had a fire going in the fireplace while I watched the baby. But without him nearby, this time around, I had no one else to rely on really except 'Christ Alone', coincidentally one of my favorite songs written by Keith and Kristyn Getty.

The heat in the house gradually dissipated. My son and I huddled together under blankets, and I somehow, by the grace of God, got the fire going. The weather oddly and quickly warmed up, and the flooding began. As the sump pump in our basement began to overflow, I thought of my husband and how he would have wanted me not only to watch over our son well, but also to protect the house from any damage. It was my responsibility, so I assessed the basement situation, as our hyperactive toddler played nearby, completely oblivious that anything unusual was going on. I tried bailing out the overflowing sump pump water with the only bucket handy; my parents doing this as well, about eight miles away, in the basement of their home. They were the only people I thought to call right away, as I was concerned for them too. They certainly couldn't come to help me in any way. I could only pray for them, and they for me, and my son. My neighbors on our rural road were in a similar boat. Perhaps some of them had generators, but with so many trees and power lines being down, it made driving, and even walking around the neighborhood to help others, an immediate risk. I couldn't possibly ask anyone to take a chance on coming down to help us. I had heard on our little battery operated radio that the nearby town where my in-laws lived was unaffected by the storm, so I took comfort in that, but dared not reach out to them for help. The streets were not plowed, and it would have been too dangerous to even think of them attempting to drive out to our part of the city. Yet it was obvious to me, even early on in the bailing process that I could not expect to continue to do this calmly, as my son ran around getting into things he shouldn't have been getting into. Even without my rising concern for his safety, the fact was I was just *not* physically or emotionally strong enough to keep it up alone for long. Even though I felt like crying, I didn't want to upset my son.

As I tried to compose myself there in the basement of our home, I remembered a Bible story one of my teachers had recounted as she taught our little group of lady friends who would meet weekly for prayer and Bible study. It was about blessings. I believe God had kept us all safe from any electrical mishaps, as wires were fed through our house into the watery bowels of our basement. After that, it was pretty much smooth sailing, and when my husband returned at the end of the weekend, there was barely any snow left in the city. It had melted. The only evidence left from the storm were some very tired people, and power outages in some areas, and the downed tree limbs all over. Perhaps God was just doing some pruning? Anyway, my faith in the LORD was certainly strengthened as we were completely protected, even financially, with no need to even call upon our homeowner's insurance policy for any damages! Father God is Amazing and is still working miracles today!

Lisa

"And He has said to me, "My grace is sufficient for you, for power is perfected in weakness." Most gladly, therefore, I will rather boast about my weaknesses, so that the power of Christ may dwell in me." 2 Corinthians 12:9

In Mark 4:35-41 of the Bible, we read that Jesus has just settled down into the rear of a fishing boat. He and His disciples have boarded this boat to get to the other side where He is to teach. As a fierce storm develops, their boat begins to fill with rising water and is quickly sinking their boat. Afraid, the disciples wake Jesus, and are astonished that it is even possible to sleep while waves are crashing against their boat!

But this is where I have to laugh. Jesus' reply is so comical... because, well, He's Jesus and nothing rattles Him. In true, predictable Jesus form He says "Why is it you are so fearful... do you not have any faith?" He then goes on to rebuke the storm with the command of His voice, leaving His disciples exceedingly afraid that even the winds and the waves obey Him!

Let's be honest... I believe Jesus still looks down on us today asking us that same question – "Why are you so afraid?" Even when our conditions are insurmountable and we experience tremendous fear He is always with us. He is ready to calm the storm, within and without... He is Jesus... He is above all things!

REASON # 85

HE MAKES
ME SOAR

Some people are privileged enough to have their eyes opened to the spirit world. Myself, I've never experienced this vividly.

It's more like a picture that comes to mind that I visualize. But this next testimony comes from a friend, who has been given this special gift of seeing things in the spirit, that can't be seen with the natural eye. Is there a spirit world functioning side by side with the natural world… YES THERE IS! There are angels all around you, and much more going on if you could just see…and some can.

"When I was at the altar, at church one day, I started seeing eagles. They were huge with their wings at full span. At night, I also began dreaming of eagles. And then again, when I was driving my mother home one day, in East Aurora, I saw a live eagle just sitting at the side of the road. This started in November of 2017, and I still see eagles at the altar in church today."

The above testimony, given to me by my friend, reminds us that we are spirit beings just as much as we are fleshly ones. Since the Spirit of God lives in us, we are privy to the spiritual world too. Do all have their eyes opened to see these things… no. But that doesn't make it any less real! Throughout the Bible we see God opening the eyes of people to show them the spirit world if only for a moment. I'm laughing now, because I'm reminded of the story in Numbers 22 in the Bible, when God chose to open the eyes of a donkey to see an angel that was hidden from everyone else. The donkey saw a large angel standing before him, with sword drawn and blocking his way. What's funny is his rider, Balaam, couldn't see the angel at all. Confused and angry, he couldn't get his donkey to move! If God can open the eyes of a donkey to see the spirit realm then He can certainly open our eyes too!

We see this same scenario play out in 2 Kings 6:17, as Elisha's servant, trembling in fear and panic, couldn't understand why his master Elisha wasn't afraid of the impending Syrian army that was closing in on them. Why wasn't Elisha afraid? Because he could see what his servant couldn't see. Then, Elisha asked God if He would open the eyes of his servant to see that they were not alone. So God opened his servant's eyes and he saw that the mountain side was full of horses, and "chariots of fire" surrounding them ready to protect and defend! God was right by their side with an army of angels positioned to fight!

It's peculiar to some that this realm even exists, because God has not chosen for us to see this realm on a minute by minute basis... but it exists! It's functioning side by side with our own earthly realm... Pretty incredible!

Kelley

"But those who wait on the Lord Shall renew their strength; they shall mount up with wings like eagles, they shall run and not be weary, they shall walk and not faint." Isaiah 40:31

REASON # 86

HE HELPS ME
FIND MY
WAY

Years ago I was reading a book and the only thing I remembered was one word... AFRICA! I knew at that moment I was going to Africa. I didn't know when, how, or why, I just knew I was going. And many years later I did just that...

It was 2012 and a young man by the name of Matt Sorger came to our church to minister for a weekend. At the end of the third night, he announced his ministry was going to Mozambique Africa to be with Heidi and Roland Baker, founders of Iris Ministries. He opened up the invitation for anyone to go. There was that word... AFRICA. Oh my gosh, I'm going to Africa! I made out the check for the down payment and gave it to Matt that very night.

As the time drew near, I realized I almost missed my flight to Newark two times, due to airline miscommunications. It was then that confusion started in my mind. These thoughts were coming loud and strong. "You know you really didn't pray about this trip?" "How do you know God is guiding you to go?" I listened to these taunting remarks and almost cancelled my trip. My hand was on the dial ready to call the ministry to cancel. Now, looking back I am so grateful I didn't!

I'm going to share with you the very beginning of my trip, for that was when the Lord showed me, He was guiding me...

As I landed at Kennedy Airport I went to the baggage claim to pick up my two heavy suitcases. I then headed towards the information desk. I needed directions to the hotel where I would be meeting my roommate, and the next day leave with a team of thirty for Africa. The man at the desk gave me directions fast, and I didn't right them down. For me that was trouble! I went out the door where I thought I was to go... it was dark, I was alone, and no one was around but me. I have to admit I was scared. I pictured people coming out of bushes and attacking me!

I started walking to the 10 plus stairs I was to climb to get to the train stop...somewhere on top. I thought to myself, "How am I at 4'10" going to walk up all these stairs with two heavy suitcases? I'll have to go up twice with one suitcase at a time." It was then that I heard a voice behind me, say "May I help you?" I turned around to see a handsome young man with an amazing radio broadcasting type voice. I said to him... "Are you an angel?" He smiled. I don't remember his response, but I said "Oh my gosh, THANK YOU!" He took my two suitcases, walked up that long flight of stairs and I followed behind him. He asked me where I was going. I gave him the name of the hotel and told him I didn't have a clue how to get there. He looked up the information on his phone and took me directly to the train station. He actually came with me on the train. As we approached my stop he said this is where we get off. He flagged down a taxi for me, paid the cab driver – tip and all, leaving me stunned and thanking him profusely. Then off I went to the hotel.

When I got to the hotel the person at the desk asked my name. He told me a gentleman called and said if I needed anything to call him at this number. I still have that piece of paper with his name and phone number on my fridge as a reminder of that day. It just so happens he really was a radio broadcaster, for Sirius in NYC. To think he delayed a special dinner with his friends so he could help me on this Thanksgiving night.

Pat Petersen

"You have made a wide path for my feet to keep them from slipping." Psalm 18:36

REASON # 87

HE IS
SOVEREIGN

God has a way of bringing us through some incredible moments in life. Some of those moments can be difficult, and brief in nature. While others will require God to carry us through the shadow of death. So it is with this next testimony. It may be short on words, but it is large on the sovereignty of God. Stories like this have the potential of turning into a tragedy, but as you will see God wasn't quite finished with this child yet...

"I was told, when I was young that I had a very high fever of 107.4. No one, not even the doctors, knew what was going on. I sustained that temperature for almost a week, and as time went by it was determined that I would need to be put into an ice bath to bring down my temperature. Nothing they tried was working. But I believe God and His angels were with me that day in the hospital room, because my temperature had unexpectedly started to come down! The miracle was that I had no brain damage or seizures as a result of my sustained high fever! I'm sure of one thing... God isn't finished with me yet!

Tammy

"Being confident in this very thing, that He who has begun a good work in you will complete it until the day of Jesus Christ! Philippians 1:6

248

REASON # 88

HE RESTORES

I want to share a testimony about my eldest daughter Paulette; how God in His great goodness and mercy interceded on our behalf and restored our relationship.

Myself, I grew up in a dysfunctional home. Though I was raised Catholic, I didn't know anything about the Bible. I just knew that there was a heaven and a hell, and I could recite the "Our Father." At nineteen I was married, but it only lasted 6 years, and I had 2 children with my husband. He was in the Vietnam War while we were dating, and I tried to break up with him, but his commander said that he would kill himself if we broke up, so when he came home on leave we married; but neither of us were in love.

At this time, I was still going to the Catholic Church, but my 2 sisters had turned to the Lord, in a deep spiritual way and said I should try it. But I really didn't think it would help me. You see, I had struggled to raise my daughter Paulette most of her life, and I didn't think anything could help our strained relationship. It was a dark time, but the Lord started to bring Christians into our life. My early years with Paulette were very difficult… she disliked me, and it started to affect the whole family. But it was at this time that I started to change spiritually. I finally accepted the invitation from my sisters to go to church, and they brought me to The

Tabernacle in Orchard Park. The people there prayed for me, and encouraged me to reach out to God during these trials. I also began to find my spiritual language with God, and began to pray in tongues. I started reading the Bible, and a lot of self-help books that encouraged me and were written by Christian authors. As a child, I hadn't grown up with much love or affection, but I started to understand that *"God is Love"*, and it really didn't matter how I grew up, it mattered that I knew I was loved now!

One Sunday morning I took my whole family to church. But my two eldest daughters, Paulette and Laurie, did not want to go back. My two younger daughters, Kim and Darlene continued to go with me though. I always went for prayer for my daughters, knowing that God was the only one who could help us. Meanwhile, Paulette continued to give me a hard time at home as she was growing up. I had to fight a spiritual battle for her life; every day praying for her salvation, and the salvation of all my family. She was drinking and taking drugs, and she was very thin. As a child she was always thin, but now she was extremely thin. I prayed Ephesians 4:31 over her "Let all bitterness, wrath, anger, clamor, and evil speaking be put away from her." This is how she felt towards me... angry and bitter. Though it seemed hopeless, I found rest for my soul in God alone. My hope comes from Him alone, (Psalm 62:5).

Then things got worse, she was pregnant and didn't know who the father was. She was drunk and on drugs and continued on a downward spiral. Her 3 choices were abortion, adoption, or she could keep the baby and we would help raise her child. I prayed that she would keep her baby and she did. Paulette and her daughter Courtney stayed with us for a year, and I kept praying that she would turn her life around. But she began working for a lady and began stealing from her, and it didn't take long before she got caught. She was placed in a holding center, and I asked God for wisdom to show me what to do. He was faithful, and showed me how to handle the situation with wisdom. The Bible tells us that He preserves the faithful, but the proud He pays back in full. (Psalm 31:23). Paulette eventually went to jail and they placed her in the Albion Correctional Center for Women. While at Albion, the other inmates were nice to her, and they all got along. God's favor was with my daughter because some of the guards were kind to her as well. Oh yeah... and she began reading her Bible while she was in jail ☺

I went to visit my daughter every other week at the prison, but the drive was lonely and most of the time the things I brought for her were not allowed, and I had to take them home with me. I felt discouraged, but I prayed all the way there and back, talking with the Lord, and crying out for His help. That help came, when the women of the church asked if I would like company when I drove up to see my daughter. My answer was YES! This was just the strength I needed! Just like Moses needed the support of Aaron and Hur to hold up his arms in the battle, I needed the support of friends to help me in this battle. I have many great memories of my sisters in the Lord, just being there in the car and riding up to Albion together. Their sweet spirit of encouragement meant a lot to me.

My daughter spent about 6 months in jail and when she was released she could not stay with me, so a good friend took her in, but that didn't last long. Finally, something broke... and Paulette began to change. She went to stay at another good friend's home, Linda Nelson, and her life began to turn around. Before she went to prison, she was working at Mighty Taco, and when she got out, they offered her, her former job back. Today, she manages that location, and is about to get married to a good man. She bought

a home in Cheektowaga, and even went to Hilbert College, earning her bachelor's degree, and then on to Robert's Wesleyan to earn a master's in Social Work!

Needless to say, I have always loved my daughter, and have waited a lifetime for this day to come, and it finally has! Today, she looks great and we talk often. We get along well and we love each other. Without the Lord we wouldn't be where we are today. I give the Him all the Glory and honor for getting us through those difficult days, and bringing us together to where we are now. To God be the Glory!

Marlene and my dearest daughter Paulette

"Who *is* he who condemns? *It is* Christ who died, and furthermore is also risen, who is even at the right hand of God, who also makes intercession for us." Romans 8:34

REASON # 89

HE ANSWERS
MY PRAYERS

What is small and furry and tan all over... Furball and Fuzzface! When my children were young, we had two adventurous hamsters to keep us busy! My children loved to take them out of their cage and play with them. We had this clear plastic ball that opened up to put them inside allowing them to roll through the house. We used to laugh as they would whisk by our feet in this see-through ball. My kids also put these little guys in my wicker laundry basket watching them climb up the sides of the basket and try to escape. But there were also times when we would have a small crises on our hands, as we chased them on foot through the house trying to catch them.

On this day though the small crises had turned into an unexpected game of cat and mouse. Fuzzface had managed to elude us in the middle of the chase. We had always found a missing hamster before, but this time he was nowhere to be found. We checked all the usual places, but the hours soon turned into days and we began to think the worst of Fuzzface. We decided it was time to step up the hunt, so we called upon the one person who knew exactly where he was – God! My children and I gathered in the middle of the kitchen, and formed a circle holding hands. I began to pray aloud that God would reveal to us the place that Fuzzface had run off too. All of a sudden, my youngest son, Corey (who prays with one eye open), began to shout… "There he is, there he is!" As we opened our eyes, running by us in the middle of the kitchen floor was Fuzzface!

We grabbed him and returned him safely to his cage. When it was all over we laughed as we recalled the sight of Fuzzface's furry little body running through the center of our circle. We also thanked God for answering our prayer the moment we petitioned Him! God is so Good! This faith building event in the hearts of my small children was precious in the sight of this mom.

Mary Genovese

"Again I say to you that if two of you agree on earth concerning anything that they ask, it will be done for them by My Father in heaven." Matthew 18:19

REASON # 90

HE IS LOVE

I t was a beautiful, sunny, spring afternoon and my driveway was full of maple tree helicopters. I had a decision to make – read my Bible or sweep helicopters? I decided to sweep helicopters. As I was sweeping, a car pulled up at the end of my driveway with a puppet monkey talking to me from the passenger's side. As I was walking down my driveway to his car, I thought, "Who is this guy?" He talked to me a few seconds about his monkey, and then asked for directions. After I gave him directions I walked around to his side of the car and let him know how much Jesus loved him. Tears started coming down his face. WOW! I shared the gospel message with him, and he received Jesus as his Savior right there in his car. I then ran to my basement to get a Bible to give him. I gave him the Bible and off he went.

Oh God, how precious is that... Sweeping helicopters... and a precious soul saved. God will direct people right into our path.

Pat Petersen

"A new commandment I give to you, that you love one another; as I have loved you, that you also love one another."
John 13:34

255

REASON # 91

HE GIVES ME A
NEW HEART

It was the last half of my Senior year in High School. Being shy left me with very few friends. Then a small group of Freshman guys started talking with me. A friendship developed as a 'Senior' taking interest in "Freshman." As they looked to me, my self-confidence grew. While trying to fit in, my life turned to a life with drugs, as I lit up my first joint. About the same time, I met a girl and we were intimate for the next three years. She was four months pregnant when we married before my 21st birthday. Drugs were still a part of my life, but considerately less. I was enjoying my life as a new husband and father.

Approximately a year later my best friend and 'drug buddy' told me how he accepted Jesus Christ as his Lord and Savior. I was raised Lutheran and knew all about Jesus, but what he told me seemed ridiculous. As far as I was concerned, I lost my best friend. Several weeks went by until one day he came to my house with a girlfriend. While hunched over a pool table and about to strike the ball, she said something to me that greatly convicted me! I KNEW she was right! Soon after that day, they invited me to some sort of meeting called "Lost and Found." It was held at a church called The Full Gospel Tabernacle. The people there sang and talked and prayed in a way I had never heard before! It was like they knew and loved Jesus personally! My friend asked me to go again the following week. It was that night that I surrendered my life to Jesus Christ and asked Him to be my Lord and Savior.

As my love and commitment to Jesus Christ grew, I realized that my wife's had not. Our commitment to God and to each other were not the same. She told me that she had been having an affair with another married man. It was like a knife went through my heart. (The same way my father had committed suicide when I was a teen.) Now I had thoughts of suicide. I had started a second job, part time, doing security at a marina. My nightly, hourly rounds allowed me to seek God and cry out to Him. I developed a new intimacy with Him. Thoughts of divorce kept coming to me but so did His Word, "...God hates divorce" (Malachi 2:16). I decided to return one Sunday to the church, "My Father's House," and after the service I was talking to the pastor's wife. She said, "There is someone I want you to meet". The woman I met introduced me to "Covenant Keepers". Covenant Keepers is an organization of Christians standing for the restoration of their marriages. While, I believed that my marriage of 12 years (with two sons) could be restored, it all came crashing down. I returned to my home one afternoon to find my wife with another man. At that horrible moment I said, "that's it for me, I am done." My life, at the time when I was working nights at the marina, became 'life changing.' This time allowed me to pray and seek God's will and direction for my life. Sadly, I made the most difficult decision to divorce (Matt 5:32). As my life continued on, my relationship with the Lord continued to grow. The relationship with the woman I met in connection with Covenant Keepers continued to grow too, and 14 years later we married. We have been through some ups and downs. The selfishness and deep-rooted anger, that I had throughout much of my life, had remained. THEN I attended the 2016 East Coast Leadership

Conference at The Tabernacle. My life began a new direction as I started to experience the presence of God like never before! As I drew closer to Him, He revealed more of Himself to me! Through the years, I am constantly learning more and more about how much God truly and unconditionally loves us! He transformed me and He has given me a completely renewed love for my wife! My daily prayer is to surrender completely to His will.

I ask Him to do whatever He needs to do in me so that His purpose for my life will be fulfilled. I desire all the spiritual gifts available in order to speak life and health to others. I desire to be a conduit of His love. "To God be the Glory!"

Earl Galati

"That I may know Him and the power of His resurrection and the fellowship of His suffering, being made conformable unto His death." "I press toward the mark for the purpose of the High calling of God in Christ Jesus." Philippians 3: 10, 14

REASON # 92

HE CAN DO
ANYTHING

Four years ago in the Fall, at one of our "Caring Hearts" prayer and worship gatherings, a women decided to bring her sister to one of our meetings. I prayed for her, and then I prayed for her baby, Joseph. He was at home with his father so she could attend our meeting. I prayed in the Spirit for what seemed like an eternity, and then we finished. I had never prayed that long for anyone. The spirit was moving strongly, and I prayed until I felt a release. As time went by, suddenly a phone kept ringing. It was a cell phone with a regular ring like the old fashioned phones had in the day. It was noticeable and a bit distracting. The woman I prayed for got up and went outside of the building for a few moments. When she came back inside she was full of awe and wonder… her baby, Joseph, had been healed while at home! Her husband called and wondered what we were doing at the prayer meeting because God just healed their baby! He was currently in therapy learning how to bend his knees and crawl. Our precious Lord healed this child - he began crawling while he was with his dad at home as we were praying… it was a miracle! All Praise goes to our Lord and Savior who Heals!

Grateful

"…For I am the Lord who heals you." Exodus 15:26b

REASON # 93

HE IS MY
EVERYTHING

I was always aware there was a God in heaven. Even as a child, I just knew He was there, even though I did not focus on Him very often. I grew up in a large family- seven children, and my parents as good Catholics, made sure we went to church every Sunday and to parochial school in our elementary school years. Life was pretty normal until I entered my teenage years where I became quite the rebellious teen, going my own sneaky way. I ended up getting pregnant and got married ten days after my 18th birthday. I had only known my husband for 4 months before my wedding day. Little did I realize that he had a terrible temper and would soon be taking it out on me.

A few months later, I gave birth to a son, and it was a struggle. All my friends were either in college, or traveling, or working and here I was, 18 years old, married and raising a family. My husband continued to vent his anger – and I felt helpless and alone. I did not think I could go to my parents, and so this became our ugly family secret.

A couple of years later, we had a daughter, a tiny bundle of discontentment. She cried all the time, and although I tried all kinds of different things, she just was not a happy baby. There was something wrong, but we did not know it at the time. When she was about 12-13 months old, she still was not walking and at first the doctors said not to worry, but when this continued into 18 months of age they realized that she could not straighten her right leg. It was at this time they told me she might have muscular dystrophy. I remember the devastation I felt when I heard those words.

I left my husband and moved in with my brother. We shared an upper apartment and there was a girl and her husband who lived in the lower apartment who had two children the same age as mine. She grew up in the same town I did, and it turns out her husband and my brother were classmates growing up. We became fast friends, and before long she started talking to me about the Lord. She told me revolutionary things like: I don't have to go to a priest; I can talk to God directly. We don't need to pray to Mary or dead saints. God loved me so much that He sent His Son to pay the price for all my sins, and nothing can separate me from His love. Those words were refreshing for my soul! I drank them in - God sent the right person at the right time to point me to the Savior. She then invited me to some revival services at her church. The first night I went, I thought they were all crazy- no one could be that happy! But she invited me again, and that night the Holy Spirit drew me in and I went forward to receive Christ. My citizenship changed, my eternal destination changed, and although I still had a sick little girl and a very challenging life, I knew that I would never be the same. I developed an intense hunger for the Word. I could not put it down! I was so excited, full of lots of questions and an inexplicable joy.

In the meantime, my husband had been asking me to come back, and making promises that things would be different. We would start a new life in Allegany County, just the four of us and raise our family in the country. It was revealed that our daughter did not have muscular dystrophy, but had juvenile rheumatoid arthritis, and after having to take much medication and wear casts and splints on her legs, she was eventually able to walk.

After a few weeks of learning many new things from my Christian friend, she pointed me to a verse in 1 Corinthians 7:13 "And if a woman has a husband who is not a believer and he is willing to live with her, she must not divorce him."

Eventually, I went back with my husband and we moved to the Southern Tier. I was hungry for Christian fellowship, and thankfully there was a Christian radio station down there. Through an interesting set of circumstances, I befriended a woman who was a believing mom, just like me, and soon I was attending church with her. Fast forward a few years and 2 more daughters, my marriage was unable to survive my husband's temper, and he ended up moving across the country to the west coast.

The Lord took good care of me and the kids, and my love for God has just increased over the years. Now I am a grandmother and have the pleasure of watching my children raise their children in the Lord. I am blessed beyond measure!

Manasseh Joy

"I am my Beloved's, and my Beloved is mine."
Song of Solomon 6:3

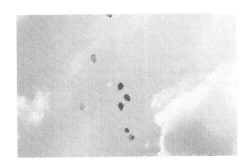

REASON # 94

HE TAKES ME INTO ETERNITY

I've Just Seen Jesus!!! In John 14 of the Bible, Jesus comforts His disciples after telling them He will one day have to leave them, "Let not your heart be troubled; you believe in God, believe also in Me. In My Father's house are many mansions; if *it were* not *so*, I would have told you. *I go to prepare a place for you*. And if I go and prepare a place for you, *I will come again and receive you to Myself; that where I am, there you may be also*." (John 14:1-3 NKJV) Through this passage, Jesus also offers us, as Believers, hope…that there is truly *eternal life* awaiting us after death. I believe this with all my heart because I've witnessed it, first-hand.

In May of 2011, my Mother suffered a major A-Fib Stroke. A-Fib is a heart condition, in which the heart beats irregularly. Thankfully, my Mother was not left paralyzed from the stroke. However, it did result in weakening on one side of her body and some slurred speech. So, my Mother was placed in Rehab at the hospital that treated her, for several weeks. Praise God, she recovered, almost fully! However, within a month of leaving the hospital, it was obvious that she was not well again. She began experiencing nausea and lost her appetite, which led to uncontrollable vomiting and fever. Her symptoms mimicked a very nasty stomach flu. Mom grew lethargic and began sleeping much of the time. After three visits to the Emergency Room, she was finally diagnosed with VRE – Vancomycin-Resistant Enterococcus. VRE is more severe than even MRSA and much harder to treat, mainly because the infected person's system has become resistant to antibiotics normally used to treat such serious bacterial staph infections. VRE also has a much lower mortality rate, particularly for those with underlying medical conditions, such as my Mother's recent stroke, which left her one kidney and heart compromised.

Following Mom's diagnosis, she was treated with various combinations of antibiotics, which helped her symptoms a bit, but weren't curing the infection. After several weeks, treatment was stopped and she was placed in palliative (comfort care), then Hospice Care. It was the most difficult experience of all, having to let her go. But, unlike our Father's sudden passing, we were granted the time we needed to say our goodbyes, and for Mom to say hers, both true blessings. A huge miracle that happened during this time was the reconciliation of our Uncle, my Father's only sibling, and our Mother. For many reasons, my Mother despised my Uncle for years. He tried to reach out to her several times throughout the years to mend the rift, but to no avail. However, one day, while my Mother lied in palliative care, my one Brother who was close to my Uncle, brought him to visit Mom. God was *in* that meeting! Both of them apologized for offending the other and *forgave each other*. A *true miracle* that healed 40+ years of bitterness and resentment! I cannot begin to tell you how happy I and my four siblings were that day! And I'm sure our Father, our Loved Ones in Heaven, the Trinity and angels were rejoicing in Heaven, too!!! Just a few days later, Mom was placed in Hospice Care. With additional comfort measures now

264

in place, Mom's body began to relax, she began to accept God's Will and let go. Watching her wither away before us was not easy but, between the caring Hospice nurses, Social Workers and Chaplains, as well as Hospital Staff and our own personal church ministers and families, we had a great support system. Eventually, Mom slipped into a coma and began her journey from this life to her new life, in Heaven.

On the day Mom passed away, the majority of our family were gathered at the hospital – 4 siblings, in-laws and grandchildren. By mid-afternoon, most went home to their families. Both my Sisters, one Brother-in-law and I stayed with Mom. We knew, between the shallow breaths, cessations of breathing and her overall countenance, it would most likely be sometime that day. Just after one Sister went outside for fresh air, Mom's breathing changed dramatically. The lulls between breaths greatly increased and each breath became much shallower. When her mouth suddenly changed from an open "O" shape, to more triangular in shape, we saw it was now her time. My Brother-in-law, who'd been a Respiratory Therapist at the same hospital for many years prior to retiring, confirmed this. He left the room to get our Sister. Just moments later, as my eldest sister and I (both born-again Christians), stood on either side of Mom holding her hand, she took her final three peaceful, slow breaths …1…2…3…and she was gone. Just like that! No struggle…just peace. As she exhaled her final breath, we saw a light vapor rise up from her, which we knew was her soul leaving her body and going to meet Jesus, in Heaven. What happened next was indelibly engraved in my Spirit and will remain with me forever. Our Mother's eyes opened and her countenance changed from blank, to a look of complete awe and wonder. Then, her mouth curled up ever so slightly on each end, as if she was smiling, and a look of complete peace and awe enveloped her. We knew, in that brief but profound moment, Mom saw Jesus. He had come to meet her and take her to live with Him forever, fulfilling His eternal promise to her, as written in the Bible she loved so much. This experience showed me death, although heartbreaking, can also be blissfully beautiful. Until you've experienced it this way, you will not understand. But, I assure you, it is true. I thank God every day our Mom had such a peaceful and serene passing over, from this life to eternity. And that we were with her, to witness it. I pray, should you ever experience the long passing of a loved one, you have the blessed opportunity to witness a peaceful crossing to forever, as my sister and I did that day. I promise, you will never be the same again! It will forever change you!!! There is a song my Mother loved to hear me sing in church. The line below from the song says it all, and I know this is how she felt that day when she beheld Jesus's face!

All that I've done before Won't matter anymore. I've just seen Jesus." And I'll never be the same again!"

Karen Weaver

Whom have I in heaven but You? And there is none upon earth that I desire besides You. Psalm 73:25

REASON # 95

HE IS ALL I NEED

The economy was down, and my son had just been excused from his job. He was also having a tough time personally and going through a divorce. At that time we were worshiping at a Roman Catholic Church. We followed the rituals of lighting candles, saying novenas, publishing prayers in the newspaper, and praying to the saints for intervention. But nothing changed.

My son was desperate for work. He had a responsibility to not only support himself but also his sons. It was at that time when I met a Pastor from a church called, "The Tabernacle in Orchard Park." He invited me to attend a Bible class, and said I could pray to God Our Father directly, and I didn't have to be bound by rituals. I took his advice and wrote down a prayer asking the Lord to bless my son with a new life of prosperity, and the love of a Christian woman. I promised Father God that I would join the church where my prayers were answered. Within 2 weeks of coming to the Tab. God granted my son a new job! And within a year, the love of a wonderful Christ loving woman to walk by his side. My son is now married, and walking in prosperity.

I joined the Tabernacle and am giving God thanks as He continues to bless my family! God is Great! Our faith and love in God alone, with no other rituals attached, was the answer to our prayers!!

Carol

"Most assuredly, I say to you, whatever you ask the Father in My name He will give you." John 16:23

REASON # 96

HE IS MY GREAT PHYSICIAN

It was Spring and I went upstairs to take a shower and I did a self-exam of my breast. I felt something in my left breast... a lump. So I called my OBGYN and he got me in right away. I prayed that my prayer offered in faith would make the sick person well; the Lord will raise him up (James 5:15). After my visit with the doctor, he sent me to get a CAT scan and it was confirmed that I had a lump in my left breast. I was scared, but I had to trust God with the final outcome. I would have a biopsy done at the Roswell Cancer Institute, one of the best in the world. When I got there they told me they would need to take a tissue sample to examine. The news wasn't good... they told me the tissue was cancerous, and I was scheduled for surgery. Removing my left breast is what I decided was the best option. They also checked my Lymph nodes to see if the Cancer had spread... Thank God it didn't! "Let love and faithfulness never leave you, bind them around your neck, and write them on the tablet of your heart (Proverbs 3:3).

I was told I would need chemo therapy for a couple of weeks, and it would make me feel sick. Though I didn't feel sick during that first week, my hair began to fall out. It really was a difficult time. I asked God to "preserve my life, Oh Lord according to Your word" (Psalm 119:107). I didn't need radiation so I was thankful for that. When I first looked at myself in the mirror, I asked God,

"Why Me?" The Lord wanted me to depend on Him. I had to wear wigs, but I didn't like them, so I decided to wear bandanas and scarfs. I didn't like the idea of having to stay home all the time, so I decided to get some fresh air and get out of the house. But I shouldn't have, because the risk of infection was greater if I came in contact with anyone who was ill. I was warned, but I didn't listen.

I went to a Bible study and sat next to a little boy who was coughing, and two days later, I got very sick. My white cells were attacking my good red cells, and I was put in the hospital in isolation for about a week. The Lord armed me with strength for the battle (Psalm 18:39). Today I am free and clear of Cancer! Thanks be to God!

Thank you Lord, Marlene

"Heal me, O Lord, and I shall be healed; Save me, and I shall be saved, for You *are* my praise." Jeremiah 17:14

REASON # 97

HE HAS ALL
AUTHORITY

"A nd the seventy returned again with joy, saying, Lord, even the devils are subject unto us through thy name." This verse is found in Luke 10:17. The reason I quoted this verse is because the story I'm about to tell you is of an encounter my son Corey and I had with some mischievous spirits, and what I did to make them flee! I'm using a verse from Psalm 91 to accompany this story at the end of my testimony because I used this particular Psalm, and the authority behind it to chase these intruders away.

Just because you're a Christian doesn't mean you have all the answers or the know how to handle every attack that comes against you. The good news is that God gave us the brethren not only to lift us up, but to help us out. We work together – that's why we are called the body! God has always led me to the right person who knew exactly what to do when I was without answers. This is exactly where I found myself. I was in the middle of a situation that I had never experienced before – my son and I found ourselves being intimidated by some evil spirits that were in our home one night. I wasn't quite sure what to do, so I called on the body of Christ! As I dialed the "700 Club" I was confident that God would lead me to someone who would be able to help me understand what I needed to do to fight this force of darkness

271

invading my home. Her counsel? "Pray Psalm 91 in every room of your house." And that's just what I did!

Let me back up a little and tell you just what happened... In the middle of the night one evening, I got out of bed to use the bathroom. It was right down the hall from my bedroom, and right across the hall from my son's bedroom. I didn't like to turn the light on in the bathroom, because it was too bright. This would have woken me up out of my half-conscious state that I wanted to crawl back into bed with. As I sat there in the pitch darkness of the bathroom, I became aware of the sound of voices surrounding me. I tried to make out the words, but it sounded more like whispering which manifested itself more in the manner of clatter than it did clarity.

By this time I had woken up to a fully conscious state, and was trying to figure out what was happening. This might seem strange to you, but I don't recall being all that frightened. I guess I felt the protection of God's presence more than the fear of the voices of those evil spirits. I remember getting back into bed, and thinking about what had just taken place. I didn't feel an urgent need to do anything, and I even began to question if there was any significance to it at all. At any rate, I began to drift off back to sleep when the sudden screams of my son Corey shrilled through the hallway and woke me up. I jumped out of bed knowing he had just come out of the bathroom. When I reached him he was in his bedroom crying out with fear, "There's someone in the bathroom, there's someone in the bathroom!" He told me of the voices he had heard. They were the same voices I had heard speak to me earlier. I stepped into the hallway and headed for the bathroom to switch on the light. Just as I suspected... it was empty. As I turned to go back into my son's bedroom I caught the sight of his lightbulb popping, and shattering to the ground. It had just burst open, and left the once lit room now dark. We were standing in silence amidst the broken glass. I wasn't quite sure what to make of all this, but I do remember feeling in control. I took my son, who was probably about five at the time, back into my bedroom, and tried to ease his fear by not making a big deal out of it. We eventually fell asleep, and began to rest in the tranquility of God's peace. After sending my children off to school the next morning I realized I needed to deal with the events that had transpired from the night before. I didn't want evil spirits wreaking havoc in my home anytime they wished, so I did the only thing I knew to do… I asked God for wisdom. He didn't lead me to a special prayer or scripture, but I did fell a burden to call the "700 Club." God was using a person just like you or me, a person who was a part of the body of Christ, to help me fight this spiritual battle. After explaining my situation to the prayer counselor she knew just where to direct my path to take the victory over these intrusive spirits. She didn't hesitate in referring me to Psalm 91. She told me to pray this Psalm aloud through every room of my house. I did just as she instructed me, and with each reading of this Psalm, the power of God began to rise up within me with great authority. So much so that I could sense the battle being won! Because of that prayer counselor's quick discernment, and my obedience in speaking God's Word into this situation, I have never encountered a visit from those mischievous spirits again!

Mary Genovese

"No evil shall befall you, nor shall any plague come near your dwelling." Psalm 91:10

The 3 Greatest Miracles of All Time...

#98 – CREATION

When we think about the greatest miracles of all time we need only look to God. He has performed some amazing wonders. Take for instance Creation… creating light and darkness. Water and earth. Trees and flowers. Animals and birds. Fish and even its worms. God has even made *us* to create. Not too long ago man was bound to the earth, but now we soar through the sky. Not long ago light came from a candle, not from a bulb. God has created artists and architects. Musicians, and singers. Seamstresses and chefs. He has created colors. Colors of people's skin. Colors of the sky and fields of wild flowers. Colors in the tapestry of a garment and a stained glass window. The color of eyes, the color of hair. He created breath in our lungs, and every organ and muscle in our body.

The sounds of a voice in an array of tongues. He has created it all. The goat and the hare. The antelope and the stallion. The songbird and the Muskellunge. What hasn't He created? It's all His. The angels, and the human soul. The solar system and the atmosphere. A coin and gold nugget. Peppermint and vanilla. Ice cream and flax seed. He made it all! A soft pillow to rest our head, and the light show of the night sky. The waves of the ocean, and the sand it curls up too. What a miracle it is to think about creation. God spoke it all into existence. He cares for it and watches over it. He keeps it running until its appointed end. He places the sound, the color, the smell, the taste, and touch of it all before us.

But His ultimate creation would be us… made in His very image. What He prepared for us on earth, pales to what awaits for us in heaven. Life is a gift, eternity is a gift, stepping into the presence of God is more than a gift. It is the beginning of forever. What more is there to say about creation, except that there's so much more we know nothing of, so much more we haven't seen, so much more we haven't experienced. So much more to come. But today we sit on this side of eternity just taking in what's before us, taking in what is seen. Let's remember we would have nothing, be nothing, and experience nothing without God. He is our creator – the creator of the heavens and the earth and all that is within it. It is a lofty thought to comprehend God and all His creation.

Too lofty for me....

#99 – FORGIVENESS

To be guilty of a crime, and not pay the consequences… that would be forgiveness. To be guilty of a crime and someone else taking our punishment… that is forgiveness. To be guilty of a crime, breaking the heart of a close friend, watching Him lose everything, watching Him as He wonders what He did to deserve our callousness, our disregard, our rejection, our defection, and then extend His hand to help us, to save us, to restore us… that's forgiveness. Is it a miracle? It is, when our crime is against the God who unselfishly, un-provokingly, head-over-heals in love with His creation, gets rejected by us and then He pardons us. Yes, it is a miracle.

What provoked Adam and Eve, when they had it all, and then gave it all up for a cheap replacement, a counterfeit; a walk on the dark side? Adam and Eve couldn't have been more wrong in choosing their allegiance to Satan, over their Father, their Creator, their friend. They couldn't have been more wrong in offering up their soul to a stranger, a deceiver, a replica, an imitation. The miracle that God still wants us, is what has me wondering, contemplating, and reflecting on why? Who are we? Who has deemed us worth the cost it would take to get us back?

Why do we still exist? Was it not enough for God to watch us give our loyalty over to another? To walk away from Him without regret? What would possess Him to rescue us? Was there something we could give Him in return? Does He think we are special? Are we that valuable? We must be. We were given a second chance without anything to offer up in exchange. In fact we were traded… a swap, His life for ours. Someone to bear our punishment, to take the penalty of our sin. Someone to bear our guilt and shame, to take our diseases, and sorrows, and the sins we committed against Him. Who would dare want to do this for us? Who would care? Only our Creator would care. Only He would want to make it right between us again… at His expense. Only He could come up with a plan to make this happen. But the price for forgiveness was high. He would have to pay for it with His own life if He wanted us back. Is forgiveness a miracle? It is to me. I know my value, and it doesn't measure up to His. This is not an even trade, I can't repay Him. I have nothing to give Him in return.

Or do I…

#100 – SALVATION

What more could we offer up to God than our hearts? It says in the Bible that there is more rejoicing in heaven over 1 person who repents, then the 99 "just people" who don't need repentance!! Salvation isn't a list of rules and regulations... It's a friendship with Jesus, and an assurance of everlasting life! I have never heard a single person say that they regretted asking Jesus into their heart, but I have heard many people say, they wish they had done it sooner!

What happens in Salvation? Well, my book is full of testimonies of the personal experiences people had as they encountered Jesus! He will change your life forever! But what actually happens...

Well... your day usually starts off something like this... it's what I call "life as usual." And Then It Hits You! The Spirit of God just hits you! You weren't expecting it, and you never saw it coming. Something has seriously just happened to you! Everything has just changed... because God happened to you!

You could have been in the middle of a conversation taking about God, and His power just fell upon you. Or you might have been crying out to the Lord and He just showed up and answered you. Or maybe the Spirit of God just fell upon you without warning. One thing is for sure, it is the best thing that has ever happened to you! Some people get healed emotionally or physically in an instant! For some, the weight of the world has just lifted off their shoulders. For others, love just poured into every inch of their soul and joy began to well up. Tears began to flow, and thoughts all became clearer; the fog has just lifted! Yesterday you couldn't have cared less about Jesus, but today you want to tell the world about Him! It doesn't matter if you are a millionaire or a beggar on the streets. The connection to God is always the same! Powerful! God Loves every soul equally! And unconditionally!

It's as if you left the room and someone else came back in your place! It's funny to think about it in that way, but it's not so far-fetched. Corinthians 5:17 says, "If anyone is in Christ, he is a new creation; old things have passed away; behold, all things have become new." Christ just enters you and nothing is the same again! It sounds a little sci-fi, but not really… Here's how Paul puts it in the Bible, "Now we have received not the spirit of the world, but the Spirit who is from God, that we might know the things that have been given to us." 1 Corinthians 2:12.

It just makes sense, that If God is a Spirit, then we will communicate with Him through the Spirit man. The Bible puts it like this… "The natural man does not receive the things of the Spirit of God, for they are foolishness to him; nor can he know them, because they are spiritually discerned." 1 Corinthians 2:14.

You don't just wake up one day and decide to think differently and be different… but when you encounter God that's just what happens! You've just receive a new perspective on life!

Could life have been meaningful before you met God? It would be if you didn't know any better. If you have nothing to compare it to, how would you know what you're missing? It's funny how we could be in the dark and not even know it. I've been there, and I never want to go back again! It doesn't hold a candle to new birth! The Bible tells us that God pursues us… we don't pursue Him. That nudge to go to church… it was placed there by God. He's knocking at the door of your heart and He wants you to know His love. The Word of God says that everyone is invited to

His banqueting table, but not everyone accepts His invitation. If you've never known Him, it won't be because God didn't reach out to you... He's reaching out to you now. We know from John 3:17 that God didn't send His Son into the world to condemn it, but to save it. That's Him.

His name is Jesus. He is God Himself who came into the world to save us. Life may go on as usual for you today, and nothing may change, but someday this world will no longer exist. You need to know that you can't save yourself... You need His Spirit. "But if the spirit of Him who raised Jesus from the dead dwells in you, He who raised Christ from the dead will also give life to your mortal bodies through His Spirit who dwells in you." Romans 8:11.

It is God's Spirit that seals us as His, and grants us eternal life!

If you want to know more about your Savior Jesus, I ask you to reach out to God in prayer. That's where it all begins. He is the originator of life, death, and everything in between. I can only take you so far... the rest is up to you and God. It's Supernatural and not something you get talked into. There is a prayer on page 33, if you are looking for the words. You may think that there are many avenues to God, but His word says "there is one God and one Mediator between God and man, the man Christ Jesus, who gave Himself a ransom for all!" 1 Timothy 2:5, 6

This is truly the greatest miracle of all time... Salvation!

One of the most impressive dialogues you'll ever read in the Bible is found in John 6:67-69. The Lord is asking His disciples if they are going to leave Him, and here's what Peter replies... "Lord, to whom shall we go? You have the words of eternal life. Also, we have come to believe and know that you are the Christ, the Son of the living God!" AMEN

Final Comments

I pray that you have experienced the love of God on the pages of this book. It has been a labor of love, and a life changing journey for me to put these 100 testimonies together. I am hoping that your life has been changed too, in the midst of all these miracles!

My next book will be filled with more amazing testimonies. I would love to hear your story, your testimony! God has done such great things for us. So, let us share them with others now!

If you have been given new hope, experienced a miracle of your own, or you have asked Jesus Christ into your heart, please tell me. I would love to write a book about the miracles that God has done while reading 100 Reasons!

Please email your testimony To: mary100reasons@gmail.com

"Now to Him who is able to do **exceedingly abundantly** above all that we ask or think, according to the power that works in us, to Him *be* glory in the church by Christ Jesus to all generations, forever and ever. Amen." (Ephesians 3:20, 21) It is obvious that God wants us to experience Him in the miraculous! He wants us to walk in Power! His Power!

This book is available on Amazon - in paperback and digital eBook. You can also order on my website: stuckonscripture.org. It is also available on Kindle, and in selected book stores.

28329464R00160

Made in the USA
San Bernardino, CA
06 March 2019